CAMBRIDGE LIBRARY COLLECTION

Books of enduring scholarly value

Linguistics

From the earliest surviving glossaries and translations to nineteenth-century academic philology and the growth of linguistics during the twentieth century, language has been the subject both of scholarly investigation and of practical handbooks produced for the upwardly mobile, as well as for travellers, traders, soldiers, missionaries and explorers. This collection will reissue a wide range of texts pertaining to language, including the work of Latin grammarians, groundbreaking early publications in Indo-European studies, accounts of indigenous languages, many of them now extinct, and texts by pioneering figures such as Jacob Grimm, Wilhelm von Humboldt and Ferdinand de Saussure.

Specimens of Hausa Literature

Hausa is an African language originating in Niger and northern Nigeria and spoken widely in West and Central Africa as a lingua franca. This 1896 anthology of Hausa texts (mainly Islamic religious verse and historical narratives) was the first publication supported by the short-lived Hausa Association, formed in 1891 to promote the study of the Hausa language and people. Under the association's aegis the author went on to produce a Hausa Grammar in 1897 and a Dictionary in 1899, contributing greatly to Western knowledge of the language, despite the fact that some in the field criticised him for his relatively short exposure to Hausa-speaking communities. With facsimile reproductions of the manuscripts at actual size, the texts collected in this book were the first examples of Hausa writing published in the West. Each text is transcribed into roman script and an English translation is given on facing pages.

Cambridge University Press has long been a pioneer in the reissuing of out-of-print titles from its own backlist, producing digital reprints of books that are still sought after by scholars and students but could not be reprinted economically using traditional technology. The Cambridge Library Collection extends this activity to a wider range of books which are still of importance to researchers and professionals, either for the source material they contain, or as landmarks in the history of their academic discipline.

Drawing from the world-renowned collections in the Cambridge University Library, and guided by the advice of experts in each subject area, Cambridge University Press is using state-of-the-art scanning machines in its own Printing House to capture the content of each book selected for inclusion. The files are processed to give a consistently clear, crisp image, and the books finished to the high quality standard for which the Press is recognised around the world. The latest print-on-demand technology ensures that the books will remain available indefinitely, and that orders for single or multiple copies can quickly be supplied.

The Cambridge Library Collection will bring back to life books of enduring scholarly value (including out-of-copyright works originally issued by other publishers) across a wide range of disciplines in the humanities and social sciences and in science and technology.

Specimens of Hausa Literature

Charles Henry Robinson

CAMBRIDGE UNIVERSITY PRESS

Cambridge, New York, Melbourne, Madrid, Cape Town, Singapore,
São Paolo, Delhi, Dubai, Tokyo, Mexico City

Published in the United States of America by Cambridge University Press, New York

www.cambridge.org
Information on this title: www.cambridge.org/9781108013253

This edition first published 1896
This digitally printed version 2010

ISBN 978-1-108-01325-3 Paperback

SPECIMENS

OF

HAUSA LITERATURE

London: C. J. CLAY AND SONS,
CAMBRIDGE UNIVERSITY PRESS WAREHOUSE
AVE MARIA LANE.
Glasgow: 263, ARGYLE STREET.

Leipzig: F. A. BROCKHAUS.
New York: MACMILLAN AND CO.
Bombay: GEORGE BELL AND SONS.

SPECIMENS

OF

HAUSA LITERATURE

BY

CHARLES HENRY ROBINSON, M.A.
TRINITY COLLEGE, CAMBRIDGE.
(STUDENT OF THE HAUSA ASSOCIATION.)

CAMBRIDGE:
AT THE UNIVERSITY PRESS.
1896

Cambridge:
PRINTED BY J. AND C. F. CLAY,
AT THE UNIVERSITY PRESS.

TO THE

RIGHT REVEREND WILLIAM BOYD CARPENTER

LORD BISHOP OF RIPON

PREFACE.

THE Manuscripts forming the present collection were obtained in different parts of the Hausa States of Western Central Africa, the first three by my brother the late Rev. John Alfred Robinson, and the remainder by myself. The issue of the present volume is a firstfruit of the work of the "Hausa Association" which was formed in 1891 "for the purpose of promoting the study of the Hausa language and people." The original MSS. are on paper of Egyptian manufacture, which had been brought by native caravans across the Sahara. The paper of the originals is much discoloured, and great credit is due to Messrs Nop and Co. of London for the skilful way in which nothing but the actual writing has been reproduced. The reproduction represents the exact size of the original MSS. My special thanks are due to the Syndics of the Cambridge University Press for having undertaken the publication of the present volume. It is hoped that its publication will be followed ere long by that of a grammar and a dictionary, both of which are in course of preparation.

C. H. R.

RIPON,
July 1, 1896.

ERRATA.

A 16. *Insert* "ki" *before* "ẓábi."

A 54. *For* "he shall not drink of the water of heaven" *read* "say to him that he is a heathen."

B 38. *For* "ḳoshi" *read* "ḳo shi."

D init. *For* "alrahmani alrahimi" *read* "errahmáni errahími."

D 77 note. *For* "horse" *read* "house."

F 25. *For* "who excels our prophets and" *read* "the excellence of our prophet which."

INTRODUCTION.

As the MSS. which form the present volume are the first published specimens of Hausa writing, it will be well to make a few general remarks in regard to the language in which they are written. The Hausa language is of special interest, first because it is perhaps the most widely spoken language on the continent of Africa, being spoken by about one per cent. of the whole population of the world, and secondly, because of the striking similarity of its structure to that of the Semitic languages and the possibility that it may prove to have had a definitely Semitic origin.

Extent to which the language is spoken.

Hausaland, or the country inhabited by the Hausa people, extends, roughly speaking, from lat. 8 N. to 14 N., and from long. 4 E. to 11 E., and includes an area of half a million square miles, the whole of which is within the British sphere of influence. This territory is supposed to contain a population of about twenty-five millions, fifteen millions of whom are believed to speak the Hausa language. Hausa is moreover the language of trade throughout the whole of the Central Soudan, and indeed the greater part of Africa north of the equator. Settlements of Hausa-speaking people are to be found in Alexandria, Tripoli, Tunis, and on the west coast at Sierra Leone and Lagos. The day will probably come when four languages, and four only, will dominate the entire continent of Africa. These will be English, Arabic, Swahili, and Hausa. English will be the language of the south, Arabic of the north, whilst Hausa and Swahili will be the languages of western and eastern tropical Africa.

The Hausa people.

The country in which the Hausa people live, although the least known, is in many respects the most interesting portion of Africa.

The reason why this country and language have remained up to the present time almost completely unknown to the general public is that

Hausaland has been, and to a large extent still is, cut off from intercourse with Europeans by two physical obstacles of more than ordinary magnitude. Of the two possible ways by which a traveller from the coast can approach this territory, the shortest and most obvious is to ascend the River Niger for 350 miles and then proceed overland on foot for about the same distance. The reason why this route has so seldom been attempted is partly because only within the present century has the lower portion of the River Niger been explored, and partly because of the great loss of life which has been experienced since the opening up of this route alike by missionaries, traders and explorers in their efforts to penetrate the interior by ascending the river from its mouth.

During the last few months special interest has been aroused in the Hausa people owing to the fact that a large portion of the troops selected to take part in our threatened war with Ashanti consisted of Hausas. About the same time an announcement appeared in the French papers to the effect that the French Government had decided to hold their newly acquired possessions in Madagascar with Hausa troops enlisted on the west coast. It might naturally be inferred from these two facts that the Hausas are a military race and fond of war for its own sake. Such however is very far from being the case. Though it is no doubt true that they excel all other tribes on the west coast, if not in all Central Africa, in their power of fighting, they excel them far more in their trading and commercial enterprise. One of their towns, Kano, has probably the largest market-place in the world, with a daily attendance of from twenty-five to thirty thousand people. This same town possesses, what in central Africa is still more surprising, some thirty or forty schools, in which the children are taught to read and write. Though about a third of the Hausa people now profess Mohammedanism, there is reason to believe that the very remarkable degree of civilization now existing in their country is altogether independent of Mohammedan influence and existed many centuries before the Mohammedan conquest of the country.

Relation of Hausa to the Semitic languages.

At first sight it would certainly seem as though Hausa had very strong claims to be regarded as a definitely Semitic language. Quite a third of the words which it contains are obviously connected with Semitic roots. The names for many of the commonest things, with which the Hausas must have been familiar from very early times, are apparently of Semitic origin.

Their pronouns, with two or perhaps three exceptions, are Semitic. The connection between Hausa and the Semitic languages—or, what here comes to the same thing, between Hausa and Arabic—is far closer than can be at all satisfactorily explained on the supposition that the former has simply been modified by the latter, as the result of the spread of Mohammedanism in the country, an event which has only occurred within the present century. As an additional reason for assuming the possibility of a Semitic origin for the language may be mentioned the fact that the general belief of the Hausa people is that in very early times their ancestors came from the far east away beyond Mecca. The difficulties on the other hand in the way of regarding it as a definitely Semitic language are very great if not insuperable. Two-thirds of the vocabulary bears no resemblance whatever to Arabic, the harsh guttural sounds of the Arabic are altogether wanting, and the existence of triliteral roots, the distinctive characteristic of the Semitic languages, is, to say the least, extremely doubtful.

In attempts which have been made to classify the modern languages of Africa it has been the usual custom to place those as yet examined under one of three groups, viz. Semitic, Hamitic and Bantu. The first includes Arabic and Aethiopic; the last, a large number of languages south of the equator, the distinguishing characteristic of the group being the absence of gender inflexion, the use of nominal prefixes for the purpose of designating class, and the use of pronominal prefixes.

The second division, the Hamitic, was formerly treated as a subdivision of the Semitic, though it is now generally regarded as distinct from it. It includes Coptic, Berber and probably Hausa. Possibly the Hottentot languages of South Africa, which, unlike the Bantu languages by which they are surrounded, possess a regular gender inflexion, bear some relation to this group.

The Hamitic Group of languages.

M. Renan, speaking of the limits of this group, says: "We must thus assign the Egyptian language and civilization to a distinct family, which we may call, if we will, Hamitic. To this same group belong doubtless the non-Semitic dialects of Abyssinia and Nubia. Future research will show whether, as has been conjectured, the indigenous languages to the north of Africa, the Berber and the Tuarek, for example, which appear to represent the Libyan and ancient Numidian, ought to be assigned to the same family.... It appears at any rate as the result of the latest explorations which have been made in Central Africa, that the Tuarek is simply Berber apart from Arabic influence, and that a distinct family of languages and peoples extends in Africa from the Egyptian oasis, and even from the Red Sea, to Senegal, and from the Mediterranean to the Niger*."

Unfortunately no student either of Berber or of Coptic has as yet had the opportunity of studying Hausa. I am myself entirely ignorant of Coptic and possess only the most elementary knowledge of Berber.

The Berber language.

Before going on to speak of the structure of the Hausa language it will be well to say something in regard to the origin and spread of Berber.

The various dialects to which the name Berber has been given are spoken throughout the greater part of Africa north of the Sahara and west of and including Tripoli. They include the Tuarek, spoken on the borders of the great desert, the Kabyle spoken in Algeria, and Guanche, the language which was in use in the Canary Islands at the time of the Spanish conquest. The present Berber dialects are the descendants of the ancient Libyan or Numidian which once prevailed throughout the whole of North Africa, to which S. Augustine referred when he wrote "in Africa barbaras gentes in una lingua plurimas novimus." The number of those who speak Berber in Algeria at the present time is 860,000. Berber is usually written in the Arabic characters, but traces of a distinctive alphabet are to be met with amongst certain of the Tuareks who speak a dialect called Tamáshek. This original alphabet, which bears no resemblance to Arabic, was probably at one time common to all the Berber dialects and was displaced when the introduction of Mohammedanism was followed by the introduction of the Koran and of the Arabic characters.

Grammatical structure of Hausa.

The following notes on the grammatical structure of the Hausa language may perhaps throw some light on its connection with Berber or other surrounding languages.

The *genitive* in Hausa is usually denoted by *n* or *na*; thus "the door of the house" would be *kofan gidda* or *kofa na gidda.* This method of forming the genitive is common to both Berber and Coptic.

* *Histoire des Langues Sémitiques*, par Ernest Renan, I. 2. 89.

Hausa possesses a regular *gender formation*, the general rule being that all words ending in *a* are feminine. These include all words denoting the female sex, in addition to a large number of others which are apparently treated as feminine simply because they end in *a*. The feminine of adjectives is usually formed by a modification of the termination, thus *tsofo* "old," fem. *tsofua*. In a few instances the Berber method of forming the feminine by prefixing *t* is met with, thus *nagari* "good," fem. *tagari*.

The *noun-agent* in Hausa is formed in a manner closely resembling the Arabic, viz. by prefixing *ma* or *mai* to a verb, substantive, or adjective. Thus *gudu* is "to run," *maigudu* "a fugitive"; *gidda* "a house," *maigidda* "the owner of a house"; *girima* "great," *maigirima* "a person who is great." The plural of such words is formed by changing *mai* into *masu*, thus *masugudu* "fugitives."

In the Semitic languages proper the *verbal stem* undergoes a series of changes by the addition of various prefixes, by doubling one of the existing consonants, or by modification of the vowel sounds. In this way some fifteen voices or changes of meaning resembling voices are obtained. In the Berber language there are ten such voices, though the changes in the verbal stem do not bear any close resemblance to those of Arabic. In Hausa there appear to be traces of four or five, but with one exception, viz. the formation of the passive voice, the changes in the sound of the words do not correspond to any uniform changes of meaning. The passive voice in Hausa is formed by prefixing *a*, *an* or *ana*; thus *kama* is "to catch," *ankama* "to be caught." There is nothing to correspond to this form either in Berber or in Coptic; but it bears a most striking resemblance to the VIIth form of the Arabic and to the Niphal of the Hebrew, both of which are used in a middle or reflexive sense. The conjugation of the Hausa verb is effected not by any change or modification of the verbal stem, but by prefixing what may perhaps be called verbal pronouns, which are the same for all verbs. Thus *fada* is "to speak," *zani fada* "I will speak," *ina fada* "I am speaking," *nika fada* or *nina fada* "I have spoken," etc. These verbal pronouns are probably compounds of pronouns with some auxiliary verb or verbs all clear traces of which are now lost.

The *numerals* in Hausa are apparently formed on a system which has ten as its base,—a fact which would tend to show that in very early times the Hausas were much more civilized than their neighbours. All the other surrounding languages, which I have been able to examine, have five as a base. In Berber the base was originally five, though at present for numbers higher than four it employs numerals similar to the Arabic. Whether however they have been at all directly borrowed from the Arabic is at least doubtful, as in Guanche (a Berber dialect formerly spoken in the Canary Islands, which is very unlikely to have borrowed from the Arabic) the numerals 5, 6, 7 and 8 are obviously Semitic. Possibly this may be the result of intercourse with Phoenician traders in very early times. In Fulah, Bornuese and Nupé, the three most important languages bordering on the Hausa, the numerals are formed on a base of five; but except in the case of the higher numerals, which have been obviously borrowed within recent times from Arabic, they show no resemblance to the Semitic numerals. In Hausa there is an original system of enumeration from one to a thousand, though from twenty upwards the numbers borrowed from the Arabic are those most commonly used. The number six (*shidda*) is the only one of the original numbers which closely resembles the Arabic.

The *personal pronouns* in Hausa are *na* "I"; *ka* "thou," fem. *ki*; *shi* or *ya* "he," *ita* "she"; *mu* "we"; *ku* "ye"; *su* "they." These, with the exception of *shi*, *mu* and *su*, bear a close resemblance to the Arabic, a much closer resemblance moreover than they bear to the Berber. *Shi* is the same in Bornuese and Hausa and has probably been borrowed by the latter from the former. The rest of the pronouns in Bornuese, as well as those in Fulah and Nupé, show no similarity to those in Hausa or in Arabic.

In addition to the coincidences above enumerated, it may be observed that the Hausa *so*, which means "time" or "times" when connected with a numeral, corresponds with the Coptic *sop*. The Hausa *fudu* "four" is the Coptic *ftu*, and the Hausa *dubu* "a thousand" may perhaps be the Coptic *thba* meaning "ten thousand."

System of transliteration adopted.

The system of transliteration which I have adopted is that originally propounded by the Royal Geographical Society. It has been sanctioned by the British Government and, with one or two unimportant modifications, by nearly all the Governments of Europe for the representation of the sound of geographical names. The general principle of the system is this: all vowels are pronounced as in Italian, all consonants as in English; every letter is pronounced, no redundant letters being introduced. I give here a table of the Hausa letters arranged in the order of the Arabic alphabet.

Names	Unconnected	Connected only with the preceding	Connected on both sides	Connected only with the following	Pronunciation in Hausa
أَلِفْ Alif	ا	ـا	. . .	. . .	
بَآءْ Ba	ب	ـب	ـبـ	بـ	English *b*.
تَآءْ Ta	ت	ـت	ـتـ	تـ	„ *t*.
ثَآءْ Cha	ث	ـث	ـثـ	ثـ	Soft *ch* as in *church*.
جِيمْ Jim	ج	ـج	ـجـ	جـ	English *j*.
حَآءْ Hha	ح	ـح	ـحـ	حـ	Strong *h*.
خَآءْ Cha	خ	ـخ	ـخـ	خـ	Hard *ċh* as in Scotch *loch*.
دَالْ Dal	د	ـد	. . .	. . .	English *d*.
ذَالْ Zal	ذ	ـذ	. . .	. . .	„ *z*.
رَآءْ Ra	ر	ـر	. . .	. . .	„ *r*.
زَآءْ Za	ز	ـز	. . .	. . .	„ *z*, pronounced the same as ذ.
سِينْ Sîn	س	ـس	ـسـ	سـ	„ *s*.
شِينْ Shîn	ش	ـش	ـشـ	شـ	„ *sh*.
صَادْ Sâd	ص	ـص	ـصـ	صـ	„ *s*, pronounced the same as س.
ضَادْ Dâd	ض	ـض	ـضـ	ضـ	„ *l*.
طَآءْ Ta	ط	ـط	ـطـ	طـ	„ *ts* (sometimes *t*).
ظَآءْ Tsa	ظ	ـظ	ـظـ	ظـ	„ *ts*, very seldom used in Hausa.
عَيْنْ Ain	ع	ـع	ـعـ	عـ	
غَيْنْ Ghain	غ	ـغ	ـغـ	غـ	English hard *g*.
فَآءْ Fa	ف	ـف	ـفـ	فـ	English *f* (in Hausa the dot is often written below instead of above the letter).
قَافْ Kâf	ق	ـق	ـقـ	قـ	English *k* (in Hausa this is often written with only one dot).
كَافْ Kâf	ك	ـك	ـكـ	كـ	*k*, pronounced the same as ق.
لَامْ Lâm	ل	ـل	ـلـ	لـ	English *l*.
مِيمْ Mîm	م	ـم	ـمـ	مـ	„ *m*.
نُونْ Nun	ن	ـن	ـنـ	نـ	„ *n*.
هَآءْ Ha	ه	ـه	ـهـ	هـ	*h*, pronounced the same as ح.
وَاوْ Wâ	و	ـو	. . .	. . .	English *w*.
يَآءْ Ya	ى	ـى	ـيـ	يـ	„ *y*.

The vowel sounds in Hausa are: ـَ Fatha, pronounced *a* or *e*; Kesre ـِ *i* or *e*; ـُ Dhamma *u* or *o*. The Diphthongs are: ـَى *ai*, pronounced as *i* in *ice*; ـَو *au*, pronounced as *ow* in *cow*.

The reader who is acquainted with Arabic will observe that ث and ض, which represent *th* and a sort of palatal *d* respectively in Arabic, are pronounced *ch* and *l* in Hausa.

In transliterating the Hausa into English I have represented the following letters thus: ذ *ẓ*, ص *ṣ*, ض *ḷ*, ق *ḳ*, ه *ḥ*. In each case the dot placed underneath the English letter does not represent any modification of sound, and the English student who is not desirous of reading the original character may therefore neglect it. That no variation of sound is intended may be seen from the fact that the letters represented by *ẓz*, *ṣs*, *ḷl*, *ḳk*, *ḥh* are constantly interchanged. Compare غزرى *gúzuri* F 67 and غذرى *gúẓuri* F 68; غسكى *gaskia* B 66 and غصكى *gaṣkia* B 37; فلول *fululu* C 36 and فضولوا *fuḷuluwa* B 154; كركتا *karkatta* D 31 and كرقت *karḳatta* D 32; حمّ *himma* for همّ *ḥimma* E 42.

ق *ḳ* and ه *ḥ* are comparatively seldom used in Hausa; most of the words in which they occur are borrowed from Arabic.

In transliterating Arabic words, which can in no way be regarded as adopted Hausa words, I have, at the cost of apparent inconsistency in the method of transliteration, represented the following letters thus: ث *th*, ض *ḍ*, ط *ṭ*. Thus عثمان is rendered *othman* F 242; رضوان *riḍwanu* F 222; لوط *loṭu* F 47. These words are pronounced by the Hausas as they would be in Arabic; to transliterate them as though they were Hausa words would therefore be to give the reader an incorrect impression of their sound.

In the case of Arabic words I have represented ع by ': thus صعود *ṣa'uda* F 191. In the case of Hausa words ا and ع are used simply as the bearers of the vowel sound. Thus the feminine personal pronoun is spelt indifferently اتا or عت; cf. A 14 and A 36, in each case *ita* appears in the transliteration.

According to the general principle of transliteration which I have adopted, an attempt has been made *to reproduce the sound* of the words, rather than to reproduce each separate letter of the original. To do both was impossible. Had I transliterated each several letter much unnecessary confusion would have been caused, the confusion being due to the lack of uniformity of transcription adopted by the Hausa scribe. Thus in B 90 we have زمانى, in B 95 زامنى; in either case I have represented the actual sound of the word thus: *zamani*.

In a few instances I have placed an accent over a vowel in order to indicate that the emphasis falls on a particular syllable. As however this emphasis differs a good deal in different localities I have made but sparing use of such accents.

In the case of words beginning with the Arabic article I have, in accordance with the principle of transliteration explained above, represented the word as pronounced rather than as spelt; thus الرحيمى F 1 is transliterated *errahími* not *alrahími*.

In the case of Arabic words which occur in the text and which cannot be regarded as adopted Hausa words, I have usually put a note to state that such is the case. In very many instances it will be noticed that in the original the points or vowels are either omitted altogether or inserted wrongly. In these cases I have made the necessary correction for the benefit of the English reader. Words which are spelt differently in different parts of these poems I have as a rule left as they stand, except in cases where an obvious mistake in transcription has occurred. The many apparent inconsistencies in spelling which will be noticed by the English reader will be found to be due to the idiosyncrasies of the different scribes, whose writing is here represented.

BIBLIOGRAPHY.

THE following is a list of the books on the Hausa language hitherto published.

Dr Barth's *Travels and Discoveries in North and Central Africa*, 1849—1855, published in five volumes in 1857, republished in two small volumes in 1890. Dr Barth, who was a native of Germany, went out as assistant to Mr Richardson, who was sent by the British Government to explore the countries lying to the south-west of the Sahara. On the death of Mr Richardson he took charge of the expedition and carried it to a successful issue. Though written in a somewhat uninteresting style, these volumes contain a vast amount of information not only in regard to the Hausas, but also in regard to several other races inhabiting the Central Soudan. Incidental notices of the various languages met with are introduced. In 1862 Dr Barth published at Gotha a work of much more interest from the linguistic point of view, *Sammlung und Bearbeitung Central Afrikanischer Vokabularien*, consisting of notes arranged in tabulated form on ten or twelve African languages, including Hausa. This work is now out of print.

Dr J. F. Schon (also of German nationality), though never able to visit any part of Hausaland proper, spent many years in the study of the language, and published several works on it, including a dictionary, a grammar, and some Hausa stories taken down by dictation from a Bornuese native who had learnt Hausa. These last, which are published by the Society for Promoting Christian Knowledge under the title of *Magana Hausa*, afford by far the best material hitherto available for the study of Hausa in England. As Dr Schon speaks of himself as having reduced to writing a hitherto unwritten language, it is evident that he was unaware of the existence of any Hausa literature. Considering the extraordinary difficulties under which he laboured in learning the language, his work is deserving of great commendation. His dictionary has been for some time out of print, but his grammar may still be obtained from the Church Missionary Society. It was published in 1862. Dr Schon also published translations of several portions of the Bible in Hausa, but these being written in Roman characters and in very unidiomatic Hausa will require a large amount of correction before they can be of any use.

Dr W. B. Baikie, who was for many years consul at Lokoja, collected some materials for the study of Hausa, which however have never been published.

J. Numa Rat, a native of Jamaica resident on the Gold Coast, printed in 1889 a short introductory grammar of the Hausa language (Waterlow and Sons). It is very short and badly arranged, but would be of some use to any one beginning the study of the language.

M. le Roux published at Algiers in 1886 *Essai de Dictionnaire de la Langue Haoussa.* This is quite the worst of the books as yet published on the language. It consists almost as much of Arabic as of Hausa, the author having apparently no first-hand acquaintance with either.

M. A. Dirr published at Paris in 1895 *Manuel pratique de Langue Haoussa,* price 6 francs. Though the author has never apparently been in any part of Hausaland, this is the best grammar hitherto published. It is of quite an elementary character and contains exercises and a short vocabulary.

The works on the Berber language which I have consulted are *Essai de Grammaire Kabyle,* by M. A. Hanoteau, Paris 1858; *Manuel de Langue Kabyle,* by M. René Basset, Paris 1887; and *Kabail Vocabulary,* by F. W. Newman, published by Trübner, London 1887.

I may perhaps conclude the list of books relating to Hausa by referring to the chapter on *The Hausa Language* in my recent work entitled *Hausaland, or Fifteen Hundred Miles through the Central Soudan* (Sampson Low and Co., price 14/-).

SPECIMENS

OF

HAUSA LITERATURE

POEM A.

A In the name of God, the Compassionate, the Merciful; and may the peace of God be upon him, after whom there is no prophet.

In the name of (Him who is) the beginning (of all things), and with the approval of Him who dwells in heaven, send help unto me (so) will I endeavour to make an attempt.

Our talk shall be judgment, whereof it is impossible to speak fully; nevertheless thou sayest, make what attempt thou canst.

It will be a day of lamentation and much crying, a day on which there shall be no salvation, though a hundred thousand cowries be offered as the price thereof.

All ye my brothers, come, let us listen to the proclamation; all ye who are Mussulmans, for I care not for the heathen.

He (a heathen) would hear what I say and would pay no attention to it, he would merely lift up his chin and bray like an ass;

He doubts the existence of pain in the next world; when he comes to the fire he will say Alas!

Thou who art puffed up with pride because of thy relations, thy kingdom, or thy property, on the day when thou meetest with the angels, thou shalt be confounded.

(Think of) that story of Hamza and his brother, one by one they went to (the place of) the unbelievers.

THIS poem is said to have been reduced to writing by a Hausa Mallam named ليما ثيديى *Lima Chidía*, who died about 30 years ago. Chidia, the place at which he lived, lies between Kano and Garimbautshi. It is a funeral song frequently sung over graves by Mallams. It consists of: Introduction 1, 2; a warning in view of the judgment to come 3—9; a comparison between this world and the next 10—22; the duties of women 23—33; conditions of entrance into heaven 34—48; and into hell 49—62; various religious duties to be observed 63—76; description of the resurrection 77—85.

1. A common Arabic opening, cf. F 1.

2. ميسما *maisama*] from Ar. سما *sama* "heaven" with Hausa nominal prefix. *ẓan*] a frequent abbreviation for *ẓani*, cf. *ban* for *bani*.

3. ميكرا *maikára*] lit. "finisher," from كرى *kari* "to finish." Words ending in *a* are with few exceptions feminine, hence we have *nata* not *nasa*.

غرغد *gorgodo*] "measure," more often written غلغد *golgodo*. For similar interchange of letters, cf. *biar* and *bial*, *kirga* and *kilga*.

POEM A.

Bismi alláḥi errahmáni errahími   wa ṣalla alláḥu ala man la nabíyi ba'dahu
Bismi ná fára da yerdan maisama   ka yi taimako a garéni ẓan tabba kokári
Ẓanchen ḳiyáma babu maikára nata   saiko ka che ka yi gorgodonka na kokári
Rana ya ki kuka da ruri maíyawa   rana da ba cheto kudinsa dubu dari
Duk ya uwána duk ku ẓo mu ji waátsi   kulu musilmi ba rua alkáfiri
Shi ni shi kan ji fáda ta baya kunuwa   saidai shi táda haba yi jaki berbera
Shi ni shi ki shakḳa aẓába lakhira   sai ya gamu da wuta yi kan che kaitaro
Mayenka deggi ko sarota dukia   rana gamu da malaiku ka sadari
Wonan karátu hamza ni da kani nasa   su suka daidaiche shikin alkáfirai

---

4. The verb is here, as frequently elsewhere, put in the present tense though its meaning is obviously future.

5. ى *ya*] should be ين *yan* "children"; *yan* is used as a sort of irregular plural of *dan*.

با روا *ba rua*] lit. "there is no water," a Hausa idiom for "I have no care for."

6. lit. "he would hear behind his ears"; *yi* is here equivalent to *kama* "as"; in the following line *yi* is used for *shi*.

7. لاخرا *lakhira*] "the future state," including both heaven and hell.

كيتروا *kaitaro*] "alas," a lengthened form of *kaito*.

8. The meeting with the angels is probably that described in D 41—46.

9. *Hamza*] a king of Ningi, not far from Kano: helped by the heathen he made an unsuccessful attack upon Kano.

شكن *shikin*] should be ثكن *chikin*.

A This life is a sowing time for the future life, everyone who sows corn wi receive a great city.

That morning shall heap up for you tobes and trousers and things good to ea such as tuo and fura.

When thou sittest down thou shalt taste of its sweetness, whenever thou sippe water thou wilt know (that one of thine enemies) is dead.

This world is like a room where we see ropes set up (for weaving) and threa is placed ready.

This world, thou knowest, is old; an old man cannot carry a load witho leaving much behind.

This world, thou knowest, is a market-place; everyone comes and goes, bot stranger and citizen.

They read (of what was to come) but refused the choice of the next world, thoug the world (*lit.* house) is old and like unto an old man who drops his loa

If thou wilt hold it fast put forth thy left hand and hold it, (it will slip fro thy hold) although thou put both thy hands on it for fear of losing it.

This world is a sowing place for the next, all who sow good deeds shall ent the great city.

This is the story of Hamza and of Ahmadu; they left the right path, the followed one which was crooked.

The Mallams are the heirs of the prophets; we ought to take their road, a roa which leads to heaven (*lit.* the city).

They (the heathen) know but the difference between white and black, the are all at strife; how can such men act like Mallams?

Their portion shall be the fire, they shall have but little to eat; they left th right path, they followed one that was crooked.

It has been said that men should gather within the house and remain at hom that they should not allow their wives to walk in the town.

---

10. ات *ita*] is properly the feminine personal pronoun, but is here frequentl used as a demonstrative; it is sometimes written عت *ita*, e.g. line 36.

11. ميافى *mayafi*] is an adjective formed by prefixing مى *mai* to the ver فى يا *ya fi* "it surpasses." مافى *mafi* is sometimes prefixed to an adjective in orde to form a comparative or to strengthen the positive; thus *mafi kunchen* "narrower or "very narrow."

12. كمن *kamin*] or كم *kam*, cf. line 64, is equivalent to كدن *kadan*.

اغنغرى *agángari*] lit. "is rolled down." The sense is somewhat obscure.

13. God is here described as the weaver of all events.

15. دنغرى *dangari*] lit. "son of the town"; cf. *dandaki* "son of the house, i.e. servant.

16. ميبرى *maiberri*] lit. "one who leaves"; it is an epithet applied to a carrie who keeps putting down his load.

Ita dúnia nana che manómi a lakhira kowa ya nómi hatsi ya kai baban gari
Ita che da safi ta kan hada maka riguna wando mayafi ga abinchi tuo fura
Kamin kazona ẓaka sha dadi nata ḳami ka kurbata ka ji woni agángari
Ita dúnia nana da kamal daki ta ki da mu ga ankáfa ragaia ajia zari
Ita dúnia nana tsofua che kun sanni tsofo ba yin kaia ba sai daíawa berri
Ita dúnia na kasua che kun sanni kowa ya ẓo ya wúche da bako dangari
Su sun karátu su ẓábi lakhira saidai gidda da ya tsofo tsofo maiberri
En ẓaka jirfáta sa hagu da ka jirfáta kaddadai ka tára hanuka don tsoro berri
Ita dúnia nana che manómi a lakhira jamáa manan gúzuri shigga babba gari
Wona karátu hamza ni da na ahmadu sun sau tafarki sun bi wodda ya fantsari
Su ni magáda anabáwa mallamai wájib mu do haiasu wanda ta je gari
Sun san fari sun san baki duka sun fada káka su ki aiki taáda mallamai
Da rabo wuta náma jiki nasa kankanni sun sau tafarki sun bi wanda ta fandari
Anche sukintsa tsakka giddansu suna tsari kaddadai su ber mátasu yawo chikin gari

---

18. منن *manan*] should be منومى *manomi* "one who sows."
غزرى *gúzuri*] lit. "provisions for the way."
19. *wona karátu*] cf. line 9 *wonan karátu.*
Ahmadu] the brother of Hamza, cf. line 9.
فنطرى *fantsari*] in line 22 فندرى *fandari* "crooked."
ود *wodda*] more commonly وند *wanda;* so line 22.
20. دو *do*] a shortened form of دوك *doka* "to take"; cf. *du* for *duka* "all."
haiasu] should be *hainyasu.*
21. The duties of a Mallam are to teach and expound the Koran, also to chant songs over the dead. The word comes from Ar. علم *allam* "to teach."
22. lit. "the meat of their body shall be little."

A Farm-work is not becoming for a wife, you know; she is free, you may nc put her to hoe grass (as a slave).
A woman that is married gives up going to three places: the market, a publi feast and the place of drawing water.
If thou hast not a boy to take her pitcher, do thou endeavour to escort he to the water in the evening.
If she desires to go to their houses, let her ask her husband; grant her per mission provided she go in the evening.
Let her take a cloth as a covering for her body, let her crouch thus wit arms folded until the conversation is ended.
When she replies let her lower her voice in speaking; let her not be hear calling fowls, speaking with wide-opened mouth.
You know that no part of a woman's body ought to be seen when she goe out, except the soles of her feet and her eyes.
The married woman who goes out with head uncovered, on the day of th resurrection the fire shall burn her;
The married woman who goes out with head uncovered, on the day of th resurrection shall be covered with a blanket of fire.
If a woman be in love with two men, they shall suffer loss in the next world on the day of the resurrection they shall rise in the form of dogs.
He who rejects a Mallam and his sayings shall be in the presence of th Prophet as a heathen.
He who fasts but at the same time eats in secret, I have no doubt but tha you may call him a heathen.
This world has been called a sowing time for the next, all who sow good deed shall enter the great city.
Whoever is stingy and rejoices in being so, the abode of fire shall be openec for him because of his stinginess.
Whoever opens the abode of fire by his stinginess will contract an incurabl disease.

---

24. *bai*] a shortened form of *ba yi*. The position occupied by women in th Hausa States is probably a better and freer one than in any other nominally Mohammedan country. Even a woman slave is seldom made to work in the fields.

كر *kar*] a shortened form of كدّ *kadda*.

25. بكى *buki*] or *biki* is properly a marriage feast.

27. كودا *kuda*] apparently equivalent to خر *khar* "as far as."

28. تن *tan*] for *ta na*, *ẓani* being feminine.

لضبا *lulubi*] is "a woman's cloth or veil" used to cover the head and the uppe portion of the body.

29. انسو *anso*] for امسو *amso* or *amsa* "an answer."

Noma ga máta bai kamáta ba kun sani   kan yar gidda che kar ka sata a kankari
Máta da ki suna ta ber taffía uku   daga kasua khar gunbuki doka rua
Kan ba ka yaro ẓa ya do tulu nata   ka yi kokári rakía rua a chikin derri
Kuda giddansu ta ki so ta yi tanbaia   ka bata yerji sai ta je a chikin derri
Ta do ẓani tan lulubi a jiki nata   a jikinta har magána ajita atatari
Anso ta kass muría chikin magána nata   kaddadai ajita yi ságara kirkira
Kana jikin mache duk yi alaura ya ki   sai ko matakai sai ido dagga gari
Mata da ki taffía da kai nata ba rufi   rana kiáma kan wuta ta babaki
Mata da ki taffía da kai nata ba rufi   rana ḳiáma ta rufu a bergo wuta
Amusan mutum bíu sun hasára a lakhira   rana ḳiáma ẓasu tashi kaman kari
Wonan da ki kí malami da fada tasa   shi ni yi ki gabba da anabi káfiri
Wonan da ki áẓumi aboyyi shi kan taba   ni babu na shakka ku che masa káfiri
Ita dúnia nana che masomi a lakhira   jamáa manan gúẓurin shigga babban gari
Kowa ya ki rowa yana murna nata   chi ni ya bude giddan wuta don gérdama
Kowa ya budi giddan wuta don gérdama   ya tarda chuta wanda da ta makankara

---

30. كان *kana*] سنى *sani* is understood, "thou knowest"; cf. 45, 52, where it is equivalent to "truly."

32. رفوا *rufu*] Instead of prefixing *a* the passive is occasionally formed by changing the last vowel into *u*; thus *rufi* "to cover," *rufu* "to be covered."

33. The dog is generally regarded as the most despicable of all animals.

34. يكى *yi ki*] for شكى *shi ki*. Mohammed, it is supposed, will act as judge at the last day to distinguish his own followers from the heathen.

36. A repetition of line 18.

37. ينا *yana*] equivalent to اينا *ina* or شينا *shina*.

38. lit. "he will meet with a disease which has no one to rub it out."

A

Whoever chooses this world rejects the choice of the next, he seizes one cowrie but loses two thousand cowries.
God is great, He displays much generosity; in the abode of the resurrection He will act as a patient man.
Of a hundred thou hast left one in this world, there are ninety-nine there in the next world.
He who has one sickness here, you know, will have ninety-nine there.
This is the reason why we are rich; if anyone gives another to eat he shall obtain deliverance in the next world.
Whatever you have given away here you will meet with in the next world, you will obtain riches which will be free from the attacks of mice, much more of ants.
Truly there are three strangers in heaven, whatever they desire they see it brought to them.
One of these gave alms and showed much generosity, he used to pray and make adoration in the evening.
The second was a man who showed honour to his parents, and maintained friendship with his brethren in the city.
The third was a man who excelled them in declaring the unity of God; whatever happened to him he said, It is the Lord (who hath done it).
A certain king shall burn in the other world unless he repent and drink the water of heaven.
The king also who ever spake deceitfully, except he repent shall not drink of the water of heaven.
All his children and his slaves who do likewise, if he restrain them not, shall be confined within the fire.
Truly there are three men who shall burn in the next world, except they repent and drink the water of heaven.
The first is the man who prayed with his body polluted; if he repent not you will meet him in company with the heathen.

---

39. ذابت *zábata*] *ta* agrees with دونيا *dúnia*, which is understood.

40. صابرى *sábiri*] "patient," from Ar. صبر "to be patient."

41. The meaning apparently is that for the good or evil actions performed in this world a man will be repaid ninety-nine-fold in the next.

43. شيس *shiyes*] should be ثيس *chiyes* "gives to eat."

44. lit. "treasures where no mouse is, much less eating of ants."

47. درجا *darajá*] from Ar. درجة *darajah* "rank, dignity."

48. توحيد *tauhídi*] "profess unity of"; II. form of Ar. وحد *wahid* "to be one."

Kowa ya ẓábata ya ki ẓabe a lakhira   shi ni ya doki wuri ya ber hauya darri
Allaḥ taála ya yi baiwa maíyawa   a giddan ḳiyáma sai mutum esṣábiri
A chikin darri daia ka berta a dúnia   tisá'in tana chan a lakhira da guda tára
Ita madaia na(n) dammuna che kun sani   tisá'in tana chan a lakhira da guda tára
Ita che dalíli samuwa muna dúnia   kowa ya shiyes ya samu tsíra a lakhira
Komi ka baiyer ka isheshi a lakhira   ajia da ba bíra bale tausangára
Kana mutun uku ni batúri a lakhira   komi su ki so sai su ganshi atatari
Wonan da ki ṣadaka da baiwa maiyawa   sai maiṣallati maiibáda da derri
Nabiusu wanda ya ba iyáyi darajá   da rukun zumunchi ya uwa a chikin gari
Näukunsu wanda ya fisu tauhídi duka   komi ya sa masa sai ya che rabba alwara
Sarki guda daia zayi kona a lakhira   saiko da tuba ẓayi sha alkauchara
Sarki da ki ku(a) che da tsalimchi duka   en babu tuba babu sha alkauchara
Yayansa nan baiyinsa na yi su duka   en bai hannasu ba ahaddasu chikkin wuta
Kana mutun uku ẓasu kone a lakhira   saiko da tuba ẓasu sha alkauchara
Wonan da ki salla gama janaba jikka   kam babu tuba ku gamashi da káfiri

---

الورى *alwara*] Meaning obscure, it is perhaps intended for الولى *alwalia* "the patron" or "benefactor," or *alwara* may be a rare Arabic word meaning "mankind"; for this meaning of the word, cf. Sadi's Bustan (ed. Graf) Introd. line 85; in this case translate "He is Lord of mankind."

49. الكوثرى *alkauchara*] *Kauchara* according to the Koran is the name of the principal river in Paradise.

51. نايى *na yi*] *na*, which is usually placed between two nouns, one of which is dependent upon the other, is here made to join the verb to the preceding noun. We should have expected *masuyi*.

احداس *ahaddasu*] from Ar. حدّ *hadd* "to confine," or "punish."

A The second is the man who always performed his ablutions with sand, thoug there was no reason for his doing so; he shall not drink of the water of heave

The third was a man whose crimes were worse than any of theirs, he was man who constantly committed adultery within the city.

If there is no purity there is no prayer, as you know; if there is no praye there is no drinking of the water of heaven.

About this saying there is no uncertainty; whoever rejects it, leave him alon that he may become a heathen.

In heaven three men will be wanting, for they rejected the right way and followe one that was crooked.

The first is a man who gave half his attention to the worship of idols; abov there is a judge mighty and powerful.

The second is a man who was a bastard, and had no father; his mothe followed a crooked path.

The third is a man who excelled them all in evil, he refused to pray fiv times (a day).

Whoever omits the times (of prayer) passes away and is destroyed, unless ther be some obvious cause.

If there be no water thou must then wash with sand in the city unless pre vented by serious sickness.

When thou hast much toil, when thou hast much business, at the time of praye leave it or otherwise it will go wrong.

God may give thee prosperity to try whether thou wilt leave the time c prayer till it is obviously past.

When such an one shall die he shall be struck with blows, so too he shal be thirsty though he drink of five streams.

When thou anointest his face with utter darkness, his tomb shall be narrowe even as the night.

Purity is necessary, as thou knowest, for one who prays; his body, his garment his place (of prayer must be clean).

There are eighteen religious duties; pious men, we understand, perform fiftee (in addition).

---

54. تيمم *taimama*] from Ar. يم *yumm* V. form. Ablutions are only permitte to be made with sand where water is unprocurable.

58. ياد *yáda*] another form of يسد *yesda* "to throw aside."

59. حكن *hukun*] from Ar. حاكم *hakim* "a judge," *m* being changed into *n*, a frequently happens before ش *ch*.

60. lit. "the second of them a bastard who, there is no father to him, he, hi mother she follows that which is crooked." This line affords a good example c Hausa construction, which, as will be seen, closely resembles the Arabic.

64. صندرى *ṣandari*] apparently the same word as سدرى *sadari*, line 8, fro Ar. سدر *sadr* "to be perplexed."

Wonan da kan rika taimama waḳti duka   kam babu huja ka che masa káfiri
Näukunsu wanda ya fisu laifinsu duka   wonan da kan rike yin zina a chikin gari
Kam babu tsarki babu ṣalla kun sani   kam babu ṣalla babu shan alkauchara
Ima fada nana babu na shakka tata   kowa ya kita ka bershi ya ẓama káfiri
A chikin giddan aljenna babu mutun uku   sun yáda ha(i)nya sun bi wanda ya fandari
Wonan da ki tsafi shina raba hankula   a bisa hukun che maiiyawa ḳaderi
Nabiyisu sheggi wanda babu uba nasa   shi ni uwa tasa ta bi wanda ta fandari
Näukunsu wanda ya fisu laifinsu duka   shi ya ki ṣalla waḳti nana su biar
Kowa ya ber lotu ya shudi ya bata   saiko da huja wanda ki ga tsaḥiri
Kam ba rua saiko da chiuta maiyawa   rana nan ka wajaba taimama a chikin gari
Ranan kaddan wahallan kani ya shagal maka   lotu da ki ṣalla ka bershi ya ṣandari
Allaḥ ya kan gamma arziḳinka da jaraba   a bisa berri loto ya shudi tsaḥira
Rana da zai mútu kan wulakanta massa   hakkana kishírua ko ya sha kogi biar
Rana ka shafa dúfu kírim huska tasa   hakkana ya kumtata ḳabarinsa kamman derri
Tsarki ga maiṣalla ku san wájib ya ki   da ẓua jikínsa ẓua tufansa ẓua wuri
Fariḷai ga ṣalla goma ni da guda tokkos   suna da ki yi mun ji sun fadi sha biar

---

66. ولاكنتا *wulakanta*] probably from Ar. ولق *walaḳa* "to strike blows."

67. "Anointing the face with darkness" refers to the sprinkling of earth upon a corpse.

حسكا *huska*] for فسكا *fuska* "countenance"; for similar interchange of letters cf. فجا *fuja* for حجا *huja*.

69. فرضى *fariḷai*] from Ar. فرض "a religious duty."

شا بيار *sha biar*] *goma* "ten" is omitted before *sha;* this is frequently done in the numerals 11 to 19.

A There are ten more good works, you know (to be done), in order that you ma excel your friend; he surpasses whoever meets him in confessing his faults
Is it necessary, dost thou ask, that thou shouldst perform thy ablutions? Ther is but one way for thee to follow.
Thou must take care before eating to say, "God is great."
But thou must not eat before saying the opening chapter of the Koran; d not pass over its contents or miss a word in saying it.
Whoever omits to read the opening chapter has broken the leg of his war-horse.
Whoever prays, but refuses to say the opening chapter, is as a man sewing white garment without thread.
It is like earth when you desire to build; if there is no water to mix with it your earth is dry.
He who doubts the resurrection in the future world let him consider how th grain that is in the ground grows up.
On the day when the sounder of the trumpet shall sound, behold a ma pouring the earth off him.
On the day when the sounder of the trumpet shall sound you will see a ma coming out of the earth.
On that day the skull shall become hot on the man who is a blasphemer, heathen.
Everyone shall rise naked, and shall utter a cry of joy; he shall be uncircumcise as a little child.
Thou wizard who wast possest of wealth in this world, thou shalt not obtai wealth like Abubekr.
He will receive wealth, he who was the messenger of the Prophet; he gav all offerings and gifts to his followers.
Let us go to the city where we shall eat without trouble of grinding; tho wilt not see any blowing underneath cooking pots in the whole city.
You will obtain a reward according to the character of your actions on earth you will come to meet with these actions in the next world.

---

70. مستحبنت *mustahabanta*] from Ar. مستحب *mustahabb* "a supererogator good work"; the word is usually applied by the Hausas to the act of bending dow and exclaiming "Allaḥ akbar," *farilai*, in the preceding line, being to hold up the han and say the same words.

71. فستا *fisata*] equivalent to فتسدا *fitasda* "to complete."

72. كبّر *kabbar*] the II. form of the Ar. كبر *kabar* "to say Allaḥ akbar."

73. اما تكنشى *ima tukunchi*] equivalent to اما تكنا *amma tukuna*.

تنغرا *chingara*] "to skip words in reading," lit. "to eat like ants" (*gara*), i.e leaving spaces here and there untouched.

75. فرى *fari*] understand *ẓani* "a white cloth."

76. All building in Hausaland is done with moistened mud; without wate building would therefore be impossible.

Mustahabanta goma ku sansu don ku wuchi sa'a	kowa ya samasa ya fikowa hamzari
Wájib ka tanbaiyi alwaḷanka ka fisata	ita che tafarki na da kan bi ita daia
Aniyar ka wájib chi dafári ka dokata	a bisa fadin kabbar ga allaḥ akbar
Ima tukunchi dafári abachi fátiha	kadda dai ka ratsa chikinta kai mata chingara
Kowa ya ki berna karátu fátiha	shi ni ya karia kafa ga doki maihari
Kowa ya ki ṣalla shina kí fátiha	shi ni ya ki dūmkin fari nasa ba ẓari
Tanfari kasa che ka kana so kai gíni	kam ba rua kubi kasanka ya shikára
Wonan da ki shakka da tashi a lakhira	ya yi tsókachi da achi a kass da ya ki tsiraa
Rana da maibusa ya busa kafo nasa	rana ka ki ga mutum a kass da ya ki zuba
Rana da maibusa ya busa kafo nasa	rana ka ki ga mutum a kass da ya ki fita
Rana kokulwa kanua tafassa suka yi	a bisa faṣabi wanda ya zamma káfiri
Kowa tsirára za yi tashi yina gudu	hakkana gaba nasa babu sha yina jínjiri
Mayi ka sámu dúkia achikinta	ai ba ka sámu dúkia yi abubekr
Shi ni ya sámata duk ya malaka annabi	ṣadaka da baiwa du ya bai almájirai
Amuje gari da muka chi ba wahalla nika	ba shi ka ga girkin tukumya du gari
Ku ku chin halli da ka aikata na dúnia	su zaka je ka ishi chana a lakhira

---

80. lit. "the skulls have made the heads to boil..."

81. ين *yina*] equivalent to *kama* "like"; cf. ي *yi* in the following line.

82. مايى *mayi*] means either "a wizard," or "a drunkard," the former is the more probable meaning.

achikinta] understand دونى *dúnia* "in this world."

Abubekr] Mohammed's companion in his flight from Mecca, afterwards one of his chief supporters.

84. غركن *girkin*] i.e. "to cook by blowing underneath a vessel placed on the fire."

85. The transliteration is somewhat uncertain: we may either read *ku ku chin* "you will obtain," or *dukuchi*, taking this as a lengthened form of *duka* agreeing with *halli*.

POEM B.

B In the name of God the author of my words; God is great, praise be to God.
There is no God but God, Mohammed his prophet is beloved.
God the one all-powerful king, he is our lord to-day and for ever.
O God our Lord, I pray to thee for that which I seek and need.
May God sanctify our work, may He give us sense and intelligence.
O God our Lord, do thou help thy servant; not on account of the thing which he is about to do.
If on account of that which he is about to do, how was it in former time when he was still unborn?
May God sanctify our work; may He make it good, not evil.
May God, our Lord, help his servant; he is the servant of his prophet, may he save (me).
He who asks is not without reason, provided he listen to that which thou showest to him.
If he asks, but does not act accordingly, he will receive judgment on the resurrection day.
The evil (*lit.* disease) of the ignorant man will take him away, even the torment of hell is not equally harmful.

THE author of this poem, as also of D, was a Mallam named Mohammed, who lived at Birnin Gwari between Kano and Bida. It consists of: Introduction 1—3; prayer for assistance in writing 4—9; the characteristics of the fool 10—14; exhortation to follow Mohammed 15—21; impossibility of choosing both this world and the next 22—31; knowledge and sight not necessarily connected 32—34; difficulties connected with the service of God 35—43; invocation for divine help 44—46; this world to be neglected in view of the next 47—52; uncertainties and troubles of the present life 53—72; our ancestors have all passed away 73—80; we ourselves shall soon die 81—90; the world is old and untrustworthy 91—112; the necessity of preparing for the future and nature of preparation required 113—129; personal exhortation 130—135; deceitfulness of this life, necessity of knowledge and discernment 136—161; the pilgrimage to Mecca and the rites to be performed there 162—175.

1. فركون *farkoun*] is apparently equivalent to *fára na* "beginner of," cf. A 2, or it may be intended for Ar. فرقان "that which distinguishes between good and evil," i.e. the Koran.

سبحان *subhána*] Ar. "praise."

2. ابن قمنا *abin ḳamna*] lit. "a thing beloved." *ḳamna* is possibly connected with Ar. قمن *ḳaman* "worthy."

POEM B.

Bismi alláḥi farkoun kalmáta   alláḥu akbar subhána alláḥi
Alláḥu la allaḥ illa alláḥu   muhámadu rasulu abin ḳamna
Jabáru wáhidi sarki allaḥ   ubangíjinmu maiyo maigóbi
Allaḥ ubangíjinmu ni ki róḳo   komi ni ki bída da bukatata
Allaḥ shi tsarkáki mamu aikimu   shi bamu hánḳali da baṣirátas
Allaḥ ubangíji ka jiḳan bawa   ba don abin da ẓashi aika ba
En don abin da ẓashi aika ni   mi ya yi chin gabban ba woshi ba
Allaḥ shi tsarkáki manna aikinmu   shi sashi ṣálihi ba mugu ba
Allah ubangíji shi jiḳan bawa   shi baiya annabi nasa shi cheto
Matan(ba)yi ba shi rassa huja ba   sai ya ḳi ji abin da ka nuna mai
En ya yi tanbaiya ban aika ba   shi ki da alhaḳi nasa ran góbi
Chiuta da jáḥili kanwa kai nai   ko gobara ba yita don bannai

---

3. مى يو مى غوبى *maiyo maigôbi*] lit. "possessor of to-day, possessor of to-morrow," line 21. *gôbi* is frequently used of the day of the resurrection, cf. line 11. Cf. Italian *domani*, which is used in the same two senses as *gôbi*.

5. بصيراتس *baṣirátas*] from Ar. بصيرة *baṣirat* "prudence."

6. جقن *jiḳan*] "help," lit. "fill"; cf. Ar. ملا *malá*, which has the same two meanings; or *jiḳan* may be intended for جنق *jinḳa* "to have pity on."

7. يى *ya yi*] if this is to be taken as two words translate as above, or *yayi* may be translated "age" or "time."

ووش *woshi*] should be اووش *awoshi* "begotten"; the argument apparently is, if God's gifts can only be obtained as the result of meritorious action, how did any man ever obtain the blessing of birth?

10. مى *mai*] for *masa*; cf. *tai* for *tasa*, line 16, *nai* for *nasa*, line 12.

12. جاهلى *jáḥili*] Ar. جاهل *jáḥil* "ignorant," an epithet usually applied to the heathen.

كنوا *kanwa*] a lengthened form of كن *kan*, denoting conditional mood.

غوبرا *gobara*] Ar. غبار *gabár* "pain."

B The ignorant man would act like a fool; leave him alone, he exceeds the fo in imbecility.
For the fool would be utterly confused, he would think that a poisonous plan was wheat.
You my brethren, draw near to the Mallams; seek knowledge, drive away dar evil (*lit.* black disease).
Follow Mohammed, trust in him, give diligence to (follow in) his path.
The medicine of the prophet is not hot; grant to him who tastes it a lessen ing of his sickness.
Whoever beholds thee, beholds part of paradise; he (Mohammed) saves him he does not detain him or make a long examination.
We follow thee, we follow God, we believe, we give to him our confidenc and faith.
We trust in thee, we love thee; blessed art thou O lord, we obtain salvatio (through thee).
I praise thee, O lord, father of Zahra, husband of Hadija, who endures for ever.
You my brethren, listen and pay attention; leave off speaking many word listen to what I say.
The regions which are divided and have never met, these will I show to yo O my relations.
Whoever has sense, he is my friend; let us talk together, let him choose wha he desires.
Let him try to take both (this world and the next); either flees away fro him, for they have never yet come together.
Mother and daughter, you choose between them; you know that you cann marry them both.
So too earth and the next world, you know that you cannot bring ther together so as to retain them.
Look carefully then thyself as to which of them thou wilt choose.

---

13. غبن *gaban*] Ar. "imbecility."

14. دف كايينى *daffa kai y nai*] for دف كينى *daffa kai nai*, lit. "would coo his own head," a Hausa expression meaning, "would be utterly confused"; cf. M Grimwig's favourite expression in *Oliver Twist*, 'I'll eat my head.'

15. بقالثوتا *bakkal chiuta*] for *bakkan chiuta;* for interchange of *l* and *n* c *kamal* and *kaman* "like."

16. سكنكشى *sakankachi*] possibly connected with Ar. سكن *sakan* "to rely upon" cf. 83 note.

17. ياجى *yaji*] lit. "pepper," so "hot as pepper."

18. بنبينى *binbíni*] sometimes written بمبينى *bimbíni* "to examine in order t discover faults in." cf. line 46.

Shi jáḥili shika(n) yi kama hauka   shima ku bershi ya fi gaban hauka
Don jáḥili shi kan daffa kai nai   guba shina tsachi alkaki che
Ku yan uwa ku gwamatsi mallamai   ku nemi shini ku kore baḳḳal chiuta
Ku bi muhamadu ku sakankachi   ku bada ḳoḳarunku ga suna tai
Annabi mágani ba yaji ba   madándani ka bashi reggi chiuta
Kowa ganika ya ga rabbo góbi   ya tsira ba riḳḳo ba binbíni
Mun bika mun bi allaḥ mun yerda   mun bada gaskia da aminchinmu
Mun dogarinka muna ḳamna   albarkachinka sidi mu samu cheto
Ina yabonka sidi uban zaḥra   mijin hadíja maiyo maigóbi
Ku yan uwa ku jini ku saurara   ku ber yawan dumi ku ji kalmáta
Mararaba da ba su gamu ḳatsu   su ẓani baiyenna maku dengína
Kowa fa hanḳalinsa aminina   en mun fadi shi ẓabi maradinai
Shi do guda guda ta tsiri mai   domi ba angamasu atara ba
Uwa dia daiansu ka ka zabi   ka suna ba ka gakasu ka amri ba
Hakka fa dúnia da giddan góbi   ka san ba ka gamasu ka rumtsi ba
Duba sarrai sarrai kaidai duba   chikinsu kowáche fa ka ka ẓaba

---

20. دوغر *dogari*] or *dogara* "lean upon"; *maidogari* is the pole to keep a door shut. Cf. also C 47.

21. زهرا *zaḥra*] The daughters of Mohammed were Rukaiya, Zeinab, Fatima, and "the mother of Kulthûm." Possibly Zahra is to be identified with the last.

22. دمى *dumi*] or *dummi* "a loud noise"; in Sokoto it is equivalent to "word" or "speech."

23. مررابا *mararaba*] an intensive form of *raba* "to divide," with prefix *mai*; or it may be intended for *masu-araba*, the *a* before *raba* being the passive prefix; "the regions which are divided" are this world and the next.

25. غدا غدا *guda guda*] lit. "one, one," i.e. both together.

27. غدنغوبى *giddan gôbi*] lit. "the house of to-morrow."

B He who seeks heaven for himself, cares not, as you know, for earth.
He who waits for abundance to eat, cares not, as you know, for a mouthful.
You my brethren, where is your saying of prayers? if you hold fast t them, they will be a gain to you.
If knowledge (within a man) perceives not, how can the eye see clearly?
If knowledge perceives, it is not the eye, as you know, which really sees.
He who has both knowledge and sagacity clouded over, leave him, he is a a blind man.
Look within at your actions; if they are (right), you shall enter into a fai reward.
You my brethren, do ye endure strife, follow with all your heart, leavin off evil.
Fight earnestly (*or*, with your heart), leave off evil; the avoidance of it is true education.
He who overcomes his own heart, bends it as a sickle is bent.
You my brethren, let us repent, let us leave off evil; if we refuse we shal not see good.
You too, let us follow the knowledge which we have in regard to action let us not vainly trample it under foot.
That which your Mallam explains to you, keep, look not closely at his work.
I myself desire nothing, wherefore I can speak without any reference to action
He who possesses knowledge but does not act (accordingly), what will he have to say on the day of the resurrection?
You my brethren gather together and say "Amen," in order that I may pray a prayer which shall be effective.
May God grant us days without sin, may He give us food and drink and abundance.
May God grant us days of prosperity, without fear, without grumbling.

---

29. تس *tas*] shortened form of *tasa; aljanna* being feminine, *tasa* is used instead of *nasa*.

30. كبكى دنغم *kabakki dungum*] *kabakki* is properly a calabash full of food, hence equals "abundance." *dungum* is equivalent to *dyawa* "very much."

31. مصلى *maṣalli*] or rather *muṣalli*, "praying." According to Abd-el-Kadr we should read مثلى *mathali* "where are your acts of such a kind that if you hold fast, etc."

32. قرقرقر *ḳurḳurḳur*] "wide-opened"; in A 29 it is written كركرا *kirkira* and applied to the mouth. The Ar. قرقرة *ḳarḳarat* denotes the cooing of a dove. Translate as above, or, "if a man perceive not that which is prudent, etc." and so in the following line.

33. جدا *jidda*] Ar. "very much" or "in earnest."

35. باطنى *bátsini*] Ar. باطن *báṭin* "interior."

Shi wonda ki bida aljanna tas kun san ba shi kullata da dúnia ba
Shi wonda ki jiran kabakki dungum ku san ba shi kullata da lauma
Ku yan uwa enna maku maṣalli en ku riḳesu sai maku anfáni
Abinda hánḳali bai gani ba kakka iddo shi ka(n) gashi ḳurḳurḳur
Abinda hánḳali ki ganiwa kun san iddo ba shi gashi jidda ba
Ya wonda hánḳali da baṣiratai su ki rufi ku bershi makafo ni
Ku duba bátsini ga aikanku en su yi áḳiba maikiyo ku shigga
Ku yan uwa ku jimri jeḥádi dai ku bida kangara ga berin ṣwabo
Ku yaḳi ẓuchia ku berin ṣwabo akalmasshita ta yi laddabi gaṣkia
Shi wonda ẓuchiata rinjayi shi ḳoshi karḳattata kama lauji
Ku yan uwa mu tuba mu ber ṣwabo em mun kia ba mu ga da kiyo ba
Ku dai mu bi shínamu da aikawa ḳadda mu tatakishi muna banna
Abinda mallaminka ya nunama riḳéshi kadda ka lura da aiki nai
Kaina na ki niffi ba kowa ba domin ni kan fada ban aika ba
Shi wonda ya yi shinni bai aika ba enna abinda zashi fadi góbi
Ku yan uwa ku taru ku che amin don ẓani adua maianfani
Allaḥ shi bamu tsarki kwanáki shi bamu chi da sha da abin yelwa
Allaḥ shi bamu kwana lafáfa da babu razana ba bibíni

عاقبى *áḳiba*] Ar. عاقبة *áḳibat* "result" or "reward." Translate as above or "if they produce a good result you shall enter (heaven)."

36. دى *dai*] may either be for *daia* "one," or it may be equivalent to *dadai* "at all," "indeed"; cf. line 40.

37. اكلمشيت *akalmasshita*] lit. "let it be avoided, it makes true education." لدبى *laddabi*] is apparently derived from Ar. ادب *adab* "a polite education," the *l* being the Ar. article; cf. *lafia*, line 47.

38. كرقتا *karḳatta*] "to bend to one side," cf. F 7, note.

42. lit. "therefore I may speak, I have not worked."

46. لافافا *lafáfa*] the more usual form is *lafia*, which is obviously derived from Ar. عافية *áfiat* "health," the *l* being the Ar. article, which has become a permanent addition to the word, as in *laddabi*, line 37.

بيبينى *bibíni*] "grumbling," usually written بمبينى *bimbíni*, cf. lines 18, 54.

B If there be food and drink and abundance and prosperity, the service of God would spread.

Were I a child of this earth, which is coming to an end, I would not pray nor make ablutions.

Why should we feel glad at a long continuance (in this world)? I have no object of desire here.

You my brethren, abandon the business of this world; whoever follows after the business of this world serves not God.

Place this world behind you, place the next world before your forehead.

Whoever follows this world is deceived, he toils after vanity.

Watch thou though thy friend sleep, be cautious as to the thing which you do.

If thou continuest silent refrain from grumbling (to yourself), meditate on that of which you are afraid.

We have a journey before us which cannot be put aside, whether you are prepared or unprepared;

Whether by night, or just before the dawn, or in the morning when the sun has risen.

That which you have, you do not really possess; make preparation before it (i.e. death) part you (from this life).

For that day shall part you (from this world), it will steal thy life, it will leave thee lying in the ground.

It will leave thy water-bearer out of pity, and your doubts and grumbling (will go) with you.

O boy, where is thy pitiful face? you are (a child) of earth and rise not from sleep.

Look carefully, behold this earth, it is deceitful, it will not continue for ever.

It is a house in which is no relaxation or rest; there is no health in it, nothing but sickness.

Everything in the world hath an end, I have seen nothing that shall endure for ever.

---

47. عبادا *ibáda*] Ar. عبادة *ibádat* "service of God."

48. lit. "I did not pray, ablutions were made."

انشافا *enshafa*] i.e. *anshafa*, from *shafa* "to anoint" either with oil or with water.

49. داديدى *dadaidai*] a strengthened form of *dadi* "sweet."

51. لاخرلك *lakhiralka*] must either be intended for لاخراك *lakhiráka* or لاخرنك *lakhiranka*.

54. ان *en*] may either be "if" or the sign of the imperative, in which case translate "continue in silence..."

56. جفجف *jifjif*] for *jijifi*, about 5 a.m. or an hour before sunrise (*azuba*);

Iẓan da chi da sha da abin yelwa da lafia ibáda kan yado
En dan ta dúnia maikariwa ba na yi adua enshafa ba
Domin tsawan ẓama mu ji dadaidai na dúnia ba na yi marádi ba
Ku yan uwa ku ber shagalin dúnia kowa bi tata ba shi ibáda ba
Ku sainya dúnia ka a baianka ku sainya lakhiralka gaban goshi
Kowa bi dúnia nan ya rudu shina dawoinia da abin wofi
Kai dai aboka kwana kana lura ka yi hánḳali abin da ka ka aika
En ka shiru kashi rika binbíni kana tuna abin da ka ki tsoro
Muna da tafia ba fasawa en ka yi shiri da iẓan ba ashiriya ba
Yala chikin derri ko ko jifjif ko ko da safi tasawal hantsi
Abinda ki da kai ba kai ka ba ka shirinka kanda ta rabika
Domi da randa zata ta rabika ta ṣachi rai ta berka kita kunchi
Ta ber majinatanka chikin tausai da ẓulumi garika da binbíni
Yaro enna ganinka abin tausai kana ta dúnia ba ka falka ba
Duba sarai sarai ka ga dúnia na(n) rudi garita ba ta ẓamma tutu
Giddan da ba natso ba hutawa ba lafia chiki nata sai chiuta
Komi na dúnia maiḳáriwa ni ban ga wonda ẓashi shi dori ba

---

hantsi being about two hours after sunrise. For the ten divisions of Hausa day cf. Dict. under *rana*.

تاساوال *tasawal*] the final *l* is here used for *n*, the sign of the genitive.

57. lit. "the thing that is with you, you yourself do not (possess)."

58. كنتى *kunchi*] lit. "untied." It should probably be كونتى *kwanchi* "lying down."

59. مجينت *majinata*] "one who gives water in time of sickness."

60. فلكا *falka*] probably refers to rising from the sleep of death. For use of word cf. D 26.

61. تت *tutu*] "for ever," also written تتل *tutul*, تتر *tutur*, and تتت *tutut*.

62. حوتاوا *hutawa*] for فوتاوا *futawa* "rest"; for similar interchange of letters cf. *huja* and *fuja*, *huska* and *fuska* A 67.

B Thou obtainest much of thy desire, thou receivest not everything that th wishest for.
Thou knowest that no man is without desire; if thou art about to accompli anything, accomplish it with prudence.
O God, do thou grant that I may accomplish my desire, may I come the city where is the lover of truth.
Whatever thou seekest as thy object of desire, ask the Lord, thou wilt n fail to get it.
God is our Lord, one to be loved; He gives to-day, he increases on the morro
Whatever the Lord gives, there is no one to take from it or to snatch it awa
You my brethren, leave off following seducers; they call you, they say you, 'shu shu shu.'
Whatever begins will come to an end, we shall not endure, the whole wor will end.
I have seen into the inside of this world, I have seen nothing to compa with the service of God.
Will the world indeed last for ever? Our prophets do they continue in it?
Thou and the world, ye shall both come to an end, and all thy possessio and thy kingdom.
Where are thy grandfather and thy ancestors? they have all passed away those who continue not.
Behold Bello, the ruler over his kingdom; what was like unto it in the regio of the Soudan?
He ruled as king, he decreased not the kingdom, he called his people to true service.
Behold Kahukaro and his kingdom, behold Bawa and Babari.
Behold and see, they were as those who continued not on earth, both the and their kingdoms.

---

64. اسوقى *asawaḳi*] from *sauḳi* "to obtain help."

دكنف *duka niffa*] "every desire," or we may read *dukan fa*, *fa* being a enclitic particle and *duka* agreeing with *guri*.

رسكا *ruska*] more commonly *riska* "to meet with" or "obtain."

66. مذن *maẓan*] for مسون *mason* "lover of." The city here referred to i the future world, cf. A 10.

67. تاب *tábi*] sometimes spelt تاف *táfi* "to be without." It is perhaps derive from the V. form of the Ar. ابى *abá* "to refuse."

69. بباوا *babawa*] a lengthened form of با *ba* "to give," or we may rea *ba bawa* "gives (to his) slave."

70. شيطانى *shaitsáni*] Hausa pl. of Ar. شيطان "evil spirit" or "tempter."

شو شو شو *shu shu shu*] a call to take part in a game.

Kai dai asawaḳi daiawan guri   ba duka niffa guri kan ruska
Ka san mutum ba shi rasa guri ba   en ẓaka yi ka yishi chikin lura
Allaḥ ka berni en chika gurina   en je madina enda maẓan gaskia
Komi ka ki bida da bukatalka   roḳi ubangíji ba ka tábi ba
Allaḥ ubangíjimu abin ḳamna   shi baka yanẓu góbi shi ḳárama
Komi ubangíji ya babawa   ba maireggi beri maiḳwachiwa
Ku yan uwa ku ber bin shaitsáni   suna kira suna yi maku shu shu shu
Komi ya faru ẓashi shi ḳari ni   ḳarḳonmu dúnia duk káriwa
Na dubi dúnia ḥal bábinta   ni ban ga taltali ya ibáda ba
Dadai ana ẓamna dúnia dankam   da annabinmu na achiki ẓamni
Da kai da dúnia ku ḳari duk   da dukialka duk da sarautalka
Enna uban ubaka da kakani   duka sun wuchi kamal ba su ẓamna ba
Duba ga bello idon malki nai   wa ya yi tasu nan sararin sudan
Ya malakita bai reggi ḳowa ba   shina kira da addinin gaskia
Duba kahuḳaro da sarauta tai   duba ga bawa ko ko babari
Ai ka ga su yi kamal ba su ẓamna ba   a dúnia da su da sarautansu

---

72. بابن *bábin*] "inside," perhaps from Ar. باب *báb* "gate."
ي *ya*] = *kama* "as," cf. line 76 and A 6.

76. On the death of Othman in 1817 his empire was divided up between his two sons, Mohammed Bello receiving the larger portion, his capital being at Sokoto.

ادن *idon*] lit. "eye of," here "chief of"; cf. Ar. عين *ain*, which is used in the same two senses.

77. الدينغسكي *addinin gaskia*] i.e. Mohammedanism. Bello's father was the means of effecting the nominal conversion of a large part of his empire.

78. Kahukaro was king of Zamfara, Bawa of Gober, and Babari of Katsena; they were all conquered and their territories rendered subject to Sokoto.

B He who first began to live (i.e. Adam), began life only on the condition that his days should have an end.
He to whom an end has been brought, how can he avoid that end?
You my brethren, consider well the times and their changes, behold that which is deserving of pity.
My brother, you know that we shall die; let us give credence, let us put aside quarrelling.
For this world is not to be trusted; thou escapest to-day, have a fear for to-morrow.
Salute the really great man; do not listen and then say, The man who tills the ground is great.
He who gives his time to farming and tilling, leave him alone, he is a man who will have great trouble.
Salute the really great who is making preparation for the last day.
Every night such spend in prayer, in saying 'Allah akbar,' in saluting the prophet.
They cast aside this world, they look not at it, they devote their attention to the service of God.
Trouble not, let go this world, do the work which belongs to you, do that which belongs to your service of God.
Behold the world, it grows old; whatever grows old will come to an end.
It is subject to the necessity of coming to an end; when (the end) comes, it will continue in a state of desolation.
When thou seest it swollen with calamity, the east and west will disappear.
Alas for the last man left, he is to be pitied for that which he will see at the end.
At that time thou mayest go and look; though thou shalt desire a place to flee to, thou shalt not find it.

---

80. فاچى *fáchi*] means either "provided that" or "up till now." Hence we may perhaps translate "the beginner (i.e. God) in olden time had himself no beginning, his days have lasted even till now."

82. زامانوا *zamanu*] from Ar. زمان *zamán* "time" or "season."

83. *ẓamai*] a shortened form of *ẓama yi*.

كنكنچى *kankanchi*] this is possibly the French *cancan* Arabicised into كنكن *kankan* "idle gossip"; or we should perhaps read *sakankachi*. Cf. line 16, note.

85. حودى *huda*] "to hoe the ground with a *fatainya*." In Hausaland this work is always performed by slaves.

86. lit. "leave him, he is a mighty man of trouble."

88. ذكرى *ẓikiri*] from Ar. ذكر *ẓikr* "to invoke the name of God"; in Hausa it is usually confined to the invocation "*Allah akbar*," i.e. "God is great."

Maifaruwa dadai bai fára ba   fáchi da kwanakinsa na ḳáriwa
Shi wonda ankawoshi da ḳáriwa   ḳaḳa shi ki shika rassa ḳáriwa
Ku yan uwa ku lura da zamanu   da jirkitansu ku ga abin tausai
Kai yan uwa ku san mutua ẓamai   mu bada gaskia mu sa kankanchi
Don dúnia ba tan yi aminchi ba   ka tsira yo kana tsoron góbi
Agaida yan maẓa bajinin gaskia   kadda ku ji ku che bajini huda
Maiḳoḳári na noma ko huda   ku bershi bajinin wahalla ki nan
Agaida yan maẓa bajinin gaski   wonda ki shiri domin góbi
Kulum derri su kwana suna ṣalla   suna ẓikiri suna eṣṣallatunsu
Sun yesda dúnia ba su duba ba   su hanḳalinsu na ga gibádasu
Ku ber kulla da ḳunchi zamani   ku ku yi ta kanku ku yi ta ibádaku
Ku lura dúnia ta tsofi   komi ya tsofa ẓashi shi ḳari ni
Tana da sharatsan tana ḳáriwa   en sun taffo ta kan rika risbawa
En ka ga kumburata ta ta afko   gabbas da yamma zata ta gurbachi
Kaito nabaia kaito abin tausai   domin abinda ẓashi gani ḳarshi
Domin da zamani taffi kai lura   ka so wurin gudu ba ka samu ba

---

الصلاتنس *elṣalatunsu*] pronounce *eṣṣalatunsu*, lit. "they (make) their salutations (to the prophet)."

89. غبادس *gibádasu*] obviously a mistake for عبادس *ibádasu*.

90. قنشي *ḳunchi*] lit. "loosen"; or we may perhaps read *kun chi*, *chi* being used as in the common expression *chi saranta* for "gain possession of" or "enjoy."

92. شرط *sharats*] an Arabic word meaning "condition" or "obligation."

سن *sun*] this is apparently a mistake for *ta*, which would refer back to *ḳáriwa*.

93. افك *afko*] "desolation"; so in line 105, possibly from Ar. افكة *afkatun*, which is defined by the Arabic lexicon Taj-el-Aroos as "a punishment whereby the dwellings of a people are overturned."

غرباثي *gurbachi*] from. Ar. غرب *garaba* "to disappear."

95. lit. "in consequence of the time go look..."

B At that time thou mayest go and look, thou shalt cry but there shall be no answer.
God is our Lord, I pray that He may not bring us to that day.
As for us, our days are days of faith, wherefore behold a place to flee to and hide in.
You my brethren, leave off this grumbling, leave off evil hankering after this world;
As thou seest that this world will be destroyed, act not deceitfully, but perform thy service to God.
Cleave thou thyself to that which will profit thee, for this world goes to destruction.
If thou seest the world about to perish and fall to ruin, work not in order to follow it or to restore it.
If thou beholdest the sun in the dawn, the morning and until evening, thou thinkest then that it will set.
I indeed tell you, my relations, the nature of this world, in order that you may be watchful.
It is altogether old, it is the garden of Satan, a cess pit, the mother of secret (evil), itself about to be destroyed.
I have considered the world and its possessions, I have seen no continuance to its dominion.
A false friend will not become true, act not thou deceitfully nor follow a fool.
This world destroys utterly him who is devoid of sense, it is as one who says, Enter, enter, make ready crime.
It is the child of evil, the constant author of deceit, it is old and tottering with age, the nurturer of disease.
The world is old, he who places it in front of his forehead is the wife of an ass.
What does he desire in this earth? He says (that he desires) both its goods and its dominion.
Alas for that which shall not endure for ever, although its beginning was fair.

---

99. بقن تكى *baḳin chiki*] lit. "black inside," so "evil thoughts"; cf. common expression *baḳin zuchia*, lit. "black heart."

101. عيود *'aiauda*] probably from Ar. عود *'aud* "repetition."

102. رزبا *rizba*] cf. line 92, where it is written رسباوى *risbawa*. It is perhaps from Ar. رسب *rasaba* "to sink down."

105. دنان *dunana*] a contracted form of دونيانن *dúnia nana*, cf. line 110, etc. عوالرف *uwal rufi*] for *uwan rufi*; for this use of *uwa* cf. *uwal deffi* "poisonous."

Domin da zamani taffi kai lura   ka yi kururua ba amsa ba
Allaḥ ubangíjinmu ni ki roḳo   kadda shi kaimu wonan kwanáki
Mu namu kwanáki na aminchi ni   don ga wurin gudu da naboiiwa
Ku yan uwa ku ber wani bimbíni   ku ber baḳin chiki don dúnia nan
En ka ga zamani ya gurbachi   kadda ka rikichi yi ibádaka
Kai dai aiauda kanka ga anfáni   don dúnia ta je ta ta lalachi
En ka ga ta machi da da rizbata   ba aika don ka bita ka raia ba
En ka ga ṣafia rana hantsi   hal ta aṣar kana zetto fádawa
Ni dai ina gaia maku dengína   halli na dúnia don ku yi lura
Dunana tsofua gonan shaitan   salga uwal rufi maiafkawa
Na duba dúnia hal samunta   ni ban ga tabetta ba ga mulkinta
Ḳaria aboka ba ta ẓama gaski   ḳadda ka rikechi ka bi shashasha
Dúnia dunana bada magagachi   ki maishiggo shiggo da shirin ẓanba
Ta dan tsulama mairikichi tutut   agaga tsofua gonal chiuta
Dunana tsofua matal jakai   wodanda sunka sata gaban goshi
Shi mi akayi kwadai gun dúniana   wai dukia da su da sarotanta
Kaito abinda ba shi ẓama tutut   koda shina da kyaun farawa

---

106. تبتا *tabetta*] probably from Ar. ثبت "to persevere."

108. بد *bada*] according to Abd-el-Kadr this is here equivalent to *bata*, another form of *bachi* "to destroy."

ذنبا *ẓanba*] from Ar. ذنب *ẓanb* "a crime."

109. ظلام *tsulama*] probably from Ar. ظلم *tsulm* "injustice," or it may be intended for ذلمى *ẓulumi*, cf. line 59.

111. lit. "he, what desire hath been wrought in this earth."

B My boy, I bid you be watchful, let it (the world) flee away, refuse t hold it back.

Accomplish deeds fit for the next world, make much preparation; leave alon the things that belong to this world, which is to come to an end.

Give up delaying and saying, It will do when you are old; death will com before you are old.

Did a young man ever drive death away, or does not the infant carried o its mother's back die?.

Mayest thou have much prudence, so that you may observe; the boy an the old man both die in this world.

Death is the boundary (of life) and the author of separation, it is almight and causes men to lie stretched out as in the tomb.

You toil after many objects of desire, death will come unperceived, and wi take thee away.

It will in no wise admit of delay, it is meditating coming next year, perhaps to-morrow.

When it comes, it draws near to a man; his day of earthly life is ended.

Thy days on earth are numbered, thou canst not pass them nor shorten them

Leave the things of earth, they are of no use; man is like one who come and remains not.

As nothing shall continue for ever, take not up that concerning which tho art in doubt.

Leave thy possessions, listen to that which is really good; be diligent, mak preparation for the last day.

Leave the world to perish, whoever follows it will suffer loss (on) the resu rection day.

He who is on a hill sees all round; he beholds, but does not enter the pit.

He whom you see doing no service, leave him alone, the world has deceived hin

He continues uselessly in the world; he is as one who comes and remains no

---

113. زاموا *zámiwa*] "to hold back," from Ar. زمّ *zamm* "to bridle a camel."

114. شرشريا *shirshirya*] an intensive form of شريا *shiria* "to make ready."

116. غيا *goia*] "to carry a child on the back." Infants are always carried th in Hausaland, bound to the mother by a fold of cloth.

117. lit. "thy prudence is complete, behold."

118. سداد *sadáda*] probably the same as سندوا *sandua* "to creep along u perceived," or it may be connected with Ar. سدّ *sadda* "to close in" or "act as boundary to."

الجبار *aljabbaru*] from Ar. جبار *jabbár* "mighty," an epithet usually applied to Go

غشي *gichi*] "to lie stretched out motionless either in sleep or in death."

Yaro ina gaia maka kai lurà   berri sukua kana ḳi zámiwa
Ka yi ta lakhira ka ka shirshirya   ber ta dúnia maiḳáriwa
Berri jira ka che sai ka tsofi   akanmache gabban ba tsofi ba
Dadai ḳurichia na kareta   da jinjiri ba shi mutu goia ba
Da hanḳalika ya chika kai lura   yaro shi kan machi tsofo na nan
Sadáda mutua sarikin rabo   ta aljabbaru sainya mutum gichi
Kuna nan dunia díawan guri   ta kan taffo sadáda ta figeka
Ita datsai ba tan yi ta fasa ba   makáda maizachi badi ko góbi
Yawanda ta taffo ta rabeshi   ranan ta dúnia tasa ta wanyi
Kwananka dúnia madudai ni   ba ka wuchesu ma ka kasasu
Ka ber ta dúnia ba anfáni   shi ma kamal maso bai ẓamna ba
Domin abinda ba shi ẓama tutuk   kadda ka do abinda ka ka damu
Ku ber ta dukia ku ji dadadai   ku yi ḳoḳári ku shiria giddan góbi
Ku berta dúnia lalatachi   kowa bi tata shi rubushi góbi
Shi wonda ki tudu na dorarai   shina gani ba shi shigga rami ba
Shi wonda ka ga ba shi ibáda ba   ku bershi dúnia tasa ta rudai
Ya ẓamna dúnia ba anfáni   shi ma kamal maso bai ẓamna ba

---

119. دونيا *dunia*] probably for دوينيا *dawoinia* "to toil after," cf. line 52.

120. دطى *datsai*] for دادى *dadai*, cf. line 116.

مكاد *makáda*] Ar. "being on the point of doing anything."

122. معدودى *madudai*] from Ar. عدّ *adda* "to reckon up."

123. مسو *maso*] should be مذوا *maẓo* "one who comes," so also in line 129.

127. دوارى *dorarai*] better *doraro* "to look all round," perhaps connected with Ar. دور *daur* "to turn," or "to go round." For repetition of this line cf. 151.

128. رودى *rudai*] equals *rudeshi* "deceived him."

129. or "the world does not continue for any good purpose, he is as...."

B O boy, I summon you to that which will profit you. Dost thou silently refuse and givest no answer?
I have indeed regarded you so as to instruct you; (my words of) wisdom have been divided well, but thou hast not received them.
He who follows the path of the evil one, listens not to warning, and receives not correction.
He whom you see hastening after evil, follow him not, lest you become evil.
The disciple will marry one who is a disciple, desire not that he should raise up children from an abandoned woman.
I desire not that he should raise up children from an abandoned woman even if she act well, she does not act as an adornment.
The washing of clothes is worthless, apart from religion; that which is useless is worthless.
The child of the ox follows not horses; the pupil seeks after his relations.
The disciple takes no possessions which would hinder him from religion.
You fear the lightning and the roar of the thunder; whoever follows a bad woman, he and she will perish together.
We indeed tell you this, and hide it not, that we may obtain our desire on the last day.
For this world shall come utterly to an end; follow it not, lest you lose on the last day.
It deceives and overthrows the fool; thou slippest confusedly and art about to fall.
Flee thou then until there be no return; whoever enters it becomes diseased.
It would fondle you and hold you in order that it may kick you away from religion.
It enters the heart, seeking a fixed abode; thy possessions are its kingdom.

---

130. داقلى *dâḳili*] from Ar. دقل *daḳal* "to hinder" or "to forbid."

131. حلامكو *halamaku*] we should read علامكو *alamaku* (cf. MS.) "your instruction."

132. حوروا *horo*] for *foro* "correction"; cf. *huda* for *fuda*, line 85. For *gama horo* we should perhaps read *ga maiforo* "he sees not an instructor."

134. lit. "a woman disciple, her husband a disciple."

بن *bani*] probably from Ar. بنى *baná* "to build up."

جوجى *jujai*] lit. "a dunghill," an expression applied to a woman of bad character living in filth.

135. حليا *hallia*] meaning of word and of sentence somewhat uncertain, *hallia* may be for *halli* "disposition," "character," or it may be from Ar. حلية *halyat* "adornment."

Yaro ina kiranka aga anfáni   ka dáḳili shiru ba ka amsa ba
Ni dai ina ganinka halamaku   anraba hanḳali ba ka samu ba
Shi wonda ya bi túruba shaitani   ba shin ji galḳadi ba gama horo
Ya wonda ka ga na zazari banna   kadda ka bishi ku zama shaitanai
Almajira mijinta almajir   kadda ka so ya bani yal jujai
Ni ba na so ya bani yal jujai   en ta yi kiyo ba ta yi hallia ba
Banẓa ḳalai ḳalai ba addini   banẓa abinda ba shi da anfáni
Dan sanua ba shi bi dawáki ba   almajiri shi kan bida dengi nai
Ạlmajiri ba shi do kaia ba   wonda ka hanna masa addini
Ku tsarchi wolḳia tsawa na nan   kowa bi fásika su bachi tari
Mu dai muna fadi ba mu boiyi ba   domin mu samu huja ran góbi
Don dúnia da zata ta ḳarḳári   kadda ka bita ku rubushi góbi
Tana rikichi wawa gichi   ka kafia damai maiafkawa
Kai dai atsíra tun ba akoma ba   kowa shigga chiki nata ya chiutu
Ta kan yi lalaba da ta riskika   domi ta hanbarika ga addini
Tana shigga a zuchi bidan ṣabo   da dukiaka ko da sarotata

---

138. كا *ka*] should be كى *ki*.

139. فاسكا *fásika*] probably from Ar. فاسق, *fásiḳ* "profligate." In several Hausa words borrowed from Arabic the ق *ḳ* appears as ك *k*.

140. حجا *huja*] from Ar. حاجة *hájat* "desire" or "affair." In line 10 it is used for "reason."

141. قرقارى *ḳarḳári*] an intensive form of *ḳári* "to end."

ربش *rubushi*] apparently equivalent to ربتا *rabita* "lose it," i.e. the world.

142. كفيا *kafia*] properly "to slip as in soft mud."

144. رسكى *riski*] a strengthened form of *rike* "to retain," or it may be for رسكا *ruska*, cf. line 64, "to meet with."

B Consent not that it should stay for a day, much less remain over-night in your heart, reject it and drive it away.
It practises deceit in order that it may commit a crime; it takes you up now in order to make you fall.
I have prudence and am not deceived, I see not a well to fall into.
I see distinctly, there is the hyena, how can it bite me in the day-time?
I behold the water, there is no high bank, I do not topple over so as to fall.
He who is on a hill sees all round; he beholds but does not enter the pit.
Look carefully, carefully consider, if there be no knowledge there is no discernment.
You my brethren, listen, and pay attention; I have words which will profit.
For much loud talking is superfluous; listen not to it, it will bring no profit.
Thou must seek knowledge with the Mallams, (if thou wouldest) go to a future world which will be of advantage to thee.
Leave wealth alone, it is a cause of trouble, whether it be obtained or not obtained.
Search diligently for that which excels in the eyes of the prudent man search after knowledge or the service of God which belongs to it.
Thou must make preparation for the angel of death; death causes all men to lie down.
If death comes, it will not regard a kingdom, not even a Mallam, neither him nor his service.
Still less an ignorant man, who is of no use; it will snatch him away without pity.
You my brethren, let me fear lest death come to me when I have made no preparation.
I have a strong desire to go on the pilgrimage, to go to Medina, to visit the prophet.
We have great joy and gladness secretly; may God bring us to Mecca that we may show it openly.
We make the circuit, we kiss with one hand the stone, we drink water from the well Zemzem, our desire is accomplished.

---

146. بر *berri*] is here used in the sense of *bale* A 44, "much less."

ينن *yinin*] is "to stay at a place," or "to do anything till sunset."

147. رردى *rurudi*, دوككا *dokaka*] intensive forms of *rudi* and *doka*, cf. line 141.

154. فضولوا *fuḷuluwa*] "superfluous," from Ar. فضل "to be superabundant."

155. انم *anim*] for *anema*, an imperative form of *nema* "to seek."

lakhiralku] *ku* may either be referred back to *lakhira* or we may read *ku da anfáni* "you have advantage."

158. ميرابيوا *mairabiwa*] "he who separates," an epithet applied to the angel of death.

Kadda ka so yininta berri kwana   ga ẓuchianka ḳita ka koreta
Tana da rurudi don ta yi ẓanba   ta dokakaka yanzu ta gochima
Ina da hanḳali ba rudi ba   ba ni ga ríjia en fada ba
Ina gani sarai kura gata   da rana ḳa(ḳa) ta ka(n) yi ta chiji ni
Ina gani rua ba gefi ba   ba ni yi ḳunduma en fada ba
Shi wonda ki tudu na dorarai   shina gani ba shi shigga rami ba
Duba sarai sarai kai dai duba   en ba shinni ba anyi baṣira ba
Ku yan uwa ku ji ku sorara   ina da aljama maianfáni
Domin yawan dummi na fuḷuluwa   kadda ka jishi ba shi da anfáni
Kai dai anim shinni gun mallamai   ku je ku lakhiralku da anfáni
Ku berta dukia wahalla ki na   yala ta samu ko ba ta samuwa ba
Tsururin da ya fi ga mailura   neman shinni ko da ibáda tas
Kai ayi ta gúzuri mairabiwa   taro matata maida mutum kwanchi
En ta taffo ban tan ga sarota ba   hal mallami da shi da ibáda tai
Bershi fa jáḥili mutum wofi   ta kan ẓareshi ba ko da tausai
Kai yan uwa ku berni ina tsoro   kadda ta ẓo gareni ban shiria ba
Guri gareni en taffi haji ni   en je madína en yi ziarata
Muna da ḳalḳali murna boiyi   allaḥ shi kaimu mekka mu budeta
Mu yi kewoiyi muna sunban dutsi   mu sha rua a zamzamu guri ya yi

---

162. زياراتا *ziarata*] from Ar. زيارة *ziyárat* "a pilgrimage" or "visit to a shrine."

163. قلقلى *ḳalḳali*] "delight," probably from Ar. قلقلة *ḳalḳalat* "agitation."

164. دوطى *dutsi*] The famous black stone built into the outside of the Kaaba, said to have been given to Abraham by the angel Gabriel. Its colour is supposed to have been originally white and to have become black by reason of the sins of the pilgrims who have kissed it.

زمزم *zamzamu*] The well Zemzem, the water of which is drunk by the pilgrims as a cure for all diseases. It is supposed to be the well discovered by Hagar.

B O my lord, thee I supplicate; may God bring us to Mecca, this is our strong desire.
The pilgrims that are with you I pray, wait a little while for me, let us go together.
The town of Medina is ever full of light, it is the city of the son of Amina with beautiful porches.
We will perform our religious duties, we will make ready; we will go to Medina, to salute (the prophet).
It is a prosperous place, it has clouds of incense, it has the tomb of the prophet, a thing to be loved.
Behold his tomb, behold the tomb of (Abubekr), the father of Endo and Asman, behold the tomb of (Omaru) the father of Hafsi.
Let me crawl, let me place my face on the ground; within and behind, I will not decrease even the edge.
I salute, I increase my salutations, I pray, I thank indeed.
Our salvation is the Lord, and our trust is in Him; He gave us our prophet one to be loved.
He gave us his relations, his friends, and his followers, even to the present time.

I have forgotten the end of this foreign book.

---

165. ربنا *rubbana*] i.e. Mohammed.

166. محجتا *muhajata*] a shortened form of مسحجتا *masuhajata* "pilgrims."

167. دن امين *dan Amina*] Amina was the mother of Mohammed; this is the title by which the Prophet is most commonly addressed.

Medina, the burial-place of the Prophet, lies about twelve days' journey to the north of Mecca. A visit to the Prophet's tomb is not regarded as an essential part of the pilgrimage, but as a highly meritorious action whereby many sins may be expiated.

سورايى *sorayi*] a plural form of سورو *sōro* "a porch."

169. نعم *ni'am*] Ar. "favours," i.e. divine favours.

170. عندو *endo*] Abubekr's two daughters were Asma and Ayesha, *endo* must therefore be intended for the latter.

Ya rubbana gareka na ki roḳo   allaḥ shi kaimu mekka muna ḳamna
Muhajata garinku na ki roḳo   ku yi mani jinkiri amuje tari
Birni madína maihaski tutut   ta dan amina maikiyo sorayi
Mu bada fariḽinmu mu zazagi   zua madína zamu ziara nai
Tana ni'am tana habakal ḳamshi   na ḳabari annabiu abin ḳamna
Ga ḳabarinsa ga na uban endo   da asman ga na uba hafsi
En rarafi ina aza huskata   chiki da bai ba ni ragi ḳauyi ba
Ina gaisua ina deddi ḳarawa   ina addua ina shukra kadai
Tsiran ubangíji da aminchinai   shi baia annabimu abin ḳamna
Shi baia aliḥ da ṣahabai nai   da tabiina ḥal ya zua yanẓu

na manta kamal kitaba al'ajamí.

حفصي *hafsi*] i.e. Haphsa the daughter of Omar and wife of Mohammed.

The mosque which contains the tomb of Mohammed contains also the tombs of Abubekr, Omar, and Fatima.

171. i.e. "I will go to every part of the sepulchre, omitting nothing."

172: شكرا *shukra*] Ar. شكر *shakar* "to thank."

According to a traditional saying of the Prophet "one prayer in this my mosque is more efficacious than a thousand in other places, save only the Masjid-el-Harim" (i.e. the mosque at Mecca)."

174. اله *aliḥ*] Ar. "his family."

The note which is written round the illustration apparently indicates that the transcriber had forgotten the concluding part of the poem.

كمل *kamal*] Ar. "to be finished."

عجمي *'ajamí*] from Ar. عجم *'ajam* "foreigners," i.e. not Arabs.

POEM C.

This is the work of a foreign poet.

C O Lord, I the son of a weak slave, supplicate Thee that Thou woulds
save me from the evil of the world.
The evil which catches even its swift runners, much more the man in thi
world who is halt and blind.
It seizes upon Mallams, much more upon the ignorant man; O Lord sav
me that the evil come not to me.
I know not, I am myself seeking to find; whoever works without knowledge
works uselessly.
The son of the ignorant is a beast and a fool, he destroys himself, he know
nothing in the world.
The son of the ignorant is a corpse, even before he is dead; his craft durin
his sojourning on earth is in vain.
If it be said to him, Rise and seek knowledge, he would say Wait till I an
old, till indeed he would refuse altogether.
He has grown old, but finds difficulty in seeking after knowledge; like
boy he would continue seeking after this world.
He has made no preparation for heaven; he directs his desires towards thi
vain world.
He dislikes to talk much about the next world; he rejects the mercy of th
living One.

THE author of this poem was Halilu (cf. line 43), who is to be identified with Liman Chidia, the author of A. He was a disciple of Shahuni of Sanusi. His father was Sidi Muktari of Rima, his mother was a concubine named Zainabu.

It consists of: Prayer for deliverance from the evil of this world, 1—3; the character of the ignorant man, 4—14; transitoriness of this life, 15—17; the world is like a deceitful woman, 18—25; the cause of life-long sorrow, 26—30; her hostility is specially directed against the Mallams, 31—33; how to escape from her power, 34—39; prayer that blessing may rest upon the author and his relations and his teacher, Shahu, 40—49; salutations addressed to Mohammed, who was a pattern of unselfishness, 50—55.

The inscription at the head of the poem is in Arabic; for use of العجمى *al'ajamí* "foreign" cf. B, concluding note.

1. لعيفى *läifi*] from Ar. ضعيف "weak," the Arabic ض, which is always pronounced *l* by the Hausas, is here supplanted by ل *l*, cf. line 36.

POEM C.

wa ḥaẓa alkitabu sha'iri al'ajamí

Ya rabbi dan bawa läifi na barra — domin ka tsarshani ga ẓanba dúnia
Ẓanbata da ta ruski masugudu nata — balatana gurgu makafo dúnia
Ita kama mallamai berri ni jáḥili — ya rabbi tarshan kadda ta kan mani dúnia
Ni ban sani ba bida ni kaina en samasa — kowa yi aiki ba sani ya sunkwia
Dan jáḥili dabba fa ni wawa fa ni — ya tsotsi kai nasa bai sani ba ga dúnia
Dan jáḥili gawa fa ni tun bai mutu — wayansa banẓa ni zamansa na dúnia
Kur ankache masa tashi kai ta bida sani — ashitsi dada mun tsufa har shi ya kia
Ya tsofi kai nasa dan wuya ta bida sani — yaro shi kan ẓama gun bida gata dúnia
Shi ba shi yin gúzuri ga aljenna tasa — ya maida kamna tai ga banẓa dúnia
Ya sakiya ya maiyawa fa ga lakhira — ya yenki kamnata ga jinkai maihaya

---

3. lit. "O Lord save, lest the world to me." It will be noticed that 38 out of the 55 lines in this poem end with دونيا *dúnia* "world," cf. Ar. دنيا *dunya*.

5. دبا *dabba*] "a beast," probably from Ar. دابّة *dábbat* "an animal that crawls or moves slowly."

كينس *kai nasa*] "himself," lit. "his head," cf. *ni kaina* "I myself" in previous line.

7. اشطى *ashitsi*] apparently for اشثى *ashiche*, which is an irregular passive formation from ثى *che* "to say," with the personal pronoun *shi* prefixed.

8. lit. "he has grown old himself, the child of trouble in seeking after knowledge, a boy he would be in the place of search for this world"; the exact sense is somewhat uncertain.

10. ميحيا *maihaya*] "the living One," i.e. God, from Ar. حى *hay* "to live," with Hausa prefix.

C He knows not the place of the resurrection, he chooses it (i.e. the world) he unties his goods on the plain of this world.

He has not known how to bow in salutation in this world; he has continued squatting down in this world.

Alas thou fool, we pity thee here, tie up thy goods, we shall arise (and leave) this world.

He knew not that his life was about to be taken away; his thought was of continuing in this world.

Where is a state of continuance in this world? behold the fool, see his funeral in this world.

The fool would say, This world is a virgin child; the wise man perceives that the world is old.

The wise man is a good friend, he would show to us the course of this world.

If she (the world) see thee, she covers up her face, she acts deceitfully; (the fool) would say, Come thou virgin child with beautiful neck.

If she comes she takes away her veil, you see that she is old, that she has (no flesh), nothing but veins.

When thou perceivest her age thou wouldest say to her, Depart from here; she would say to thee, Thou liest, we will unite together.

If she unites to thee, she will continue to stick like gum; in every such union there is no satisfactory parting.

If she make an agreement with thee, she will not fulfil it; whoever thou art that love her, she, the earth, rejects such.

If she make an agreement with thee she will make objection to it; she makes everyone you know to deviate (from the right way).

If she give thee goods, she will snatch them away; if she give thee health be afraid of her character.

If perchance she give thee offspring, she will snatch it away; you know that every one must die.

If perchance a kingdom be yours, be afraid of her; the day of thy union with the world is not auspicious.

---

12. Both transliteration and meaning obscure. For *a kaia nan* we should perhaps read *akanyi nan* or *akan yaga nan.*

ترابع *turabi*] cf. V. form of Ar. ربع *raba‘* "to sit down cross-legged squarely."

15. اطكى *atsiki*] for اثكى *achiki,* line 12, "within."

18. ماكرى *makuri*] probably from Ar. ماكر *mákir* "an impostor."

تهو *taḥo*] = تفو *taffo* "come."

قركيا *ḳurkia*] "virgin," probably a Fulah word.

ميكى ويا *maiki wuya*] should be ميكيو ويا *maikiyo wuya* "with beautiful neck."

Bai san gidda na chiri ba ni ya ẓabesa   ya kunchi kaia nai ga fili dúnia
Bai san tsugun a kaia nan achiki nata   yai ẓamna ya yi turabi nan dúnia
Kaito ka wawa kai mu ki tausai nana   kai damna kaia ẓamu tashi dúnia
Bai san da ra nai ẓa akarbiwa tasa   shi tamaḥa tasa dawama nana dúnia
Ina da ẓama na dawama atsiki nata   kai nuri wawa ga ḳufanwa su dúnia
Wawa ka chewa yal budurua dúnia   maiḥánḳali kan gani tsofal dúnia
Maiḥánḳali shi yi aboki ṣalihi   shi kan goda muna takitaki dúnia
Kan ta ganeka ta luḷubi ita makuri   akache taḥo yal ḳurkia maiki wuya
En ta taḥo ta kori tsanan nan duka   ka ga tsofua tse sai jiwoji dúnia
En ka ga tsofa nan ka che mata kau nana   atatse da kai karia ka ki mun garwaya
En ta gamo fa da kai dada danḳo riko   ḳul ta rika dada ba rabo fa da lafia
En ta yi alḳaueli da kai fa ba tan tsikashi ba   kowa ka so nata shi ta ki ki dúnia
En ta yi alḳaueli da kai ita walwali   kun sani tana baudiwa kowa dúnia
En dukia ta baka amshiwa ta ka yi   en lafia ta baka tsorchi halli nata dúnia
En ko dia ta baka amshiwa ta ka yi   ku sani fa kowa na da ajali dúnia
En ko sarota a garéka ka tsoro tata   ranan gamun ku da dúnia ba lafia

---

20. غرويا *garwaya*] may either be the Hausa *gariwoya* "to knead together," or it may be from Ar. غروى *garwa* "eager desire for."

22. علقولى *alḳaueli*] should be written القولى from Ar. قول *ḳaul* "agreement."

23. ولولى *walwali*] from Ar. ولول *walwal* "to complain of," or "to curse."

24. امشيو *amshiwa*] "snatched away," we should perhaps read امشعو *amsh'iwa*, cf. Ar. مشع *masha'* "to carry off."

25. اجلى *ajali*] from Ar. اجل *ajal* "destiny."

C

Moreover there is no joy on the day of entry into the world; there is t no joy on the day of departing from the world.
Behold the infant on the day of its birth; it cries on the day on which enters into the world.
Look at a corpse on the day on which the dead man sets out for the ne world; we lament over him because he has parted from this world.
If we know that the dead man knows that he is forgiven, we give thank for him because he has parted from the world.
The world undertakes wars with the Mallams; she is an ignorant slave.
She mutters and speaks evil of a Mallam; she shows her strength to th ignorant.
She advances unseen to fight with a Mallam; but she seizes the child ignorance by the neck.
Whoever desires to escape, being at war with her, must abandon everythin in this world,
Except his food and drink and clothing, do you understand? thou must see for nothing in this world but clothing.
Leave off arrogance, flee from him who practises it; whoever practises it wi not obtain salvation, hearken to this.
Cleave to prayer, visit and salute the Mallams; cleave to the invocation God, it will save anyone in this world.
These are as swords to the believers, a preparation for fighting, for (th believer) trusts not in anything in this world.
Whoever follows lust and desire, obtains them, much more he who desir the possessions of this world.
O Lord, to Thee do we pray, save me in the future world; Thou guarde the son of Thy slave from the evil of this world.
Do Thou guard both my mother and my father; guard my relations from th evil of this world.

---

27. ر *ra*] a contraction for ران *rana* "day" as in previous line.

30. غافر *gáfara*] from Ar. غفر *gafar* "to pardon."

32. Translation somewhat uncertain; according to Abd-el-Kadr for دن *dun* we should read دند *dundu.* This may perhaps come from Ar. دندن *dandan* " mumble," or "to speak unintelligibly."

ذامى *zami*] probably from Ar. ذام *zám* "to blame."

33. بايبايا *baia baia*] lit. "behind, behind," an expression applied to a c creeping up behind a mouse.

تريدس *tari da sa*] for *tari da shi* "meets with him," or *taridasa* may another form of *tarasda;* the meaning will be the same in either case.

35. نشا *nasha*] shortened for ابنشا *abinsha* "drink."

Kuma babu murna ra shiggowa dúnia   kuma babu murna ra fita daga dúnia
Duba ga jariri fa randa (a)kaḥaifesa   kuka shika yi mata ra shiggowa dúnia
Duba ga gawa ra maraita lakhira   kuka mu kai mata don rabanta da dúnia
Enda muna da sani ta ka san gáfara   barka mu kai mata don rabanta da dúnia
Ita doki yakóki ta kai gun mallamai   don jáḥili bawa ta ni ita dúnia
Dunu ta kai ẓami ta kan che na mallami   karfi ta kan goda jáḥili ita dúnia
Da baia baia ta ki fada da mallami   dan jáḥili saiko tari da sa gun wuya
Kowa ki so shi fichi maiyako ki nata   ashiyerda komi nan ga dakin dúnia
Saiko abinchi nai nasha nasa kun jia   saiko tufa ka bida ga dakin dúnia
Aḳuber fululu ka ẓan gudun maiyin nasa   kowa ka yi nasa ba shi tsira akunjia
Ku riki ṣallati ka ẓan ẓiara mallamai   riki en zikir chi ki rukun kowa ga dúnia
Su ni taḳuba mumini na shirin fada   don bai amuntsiwa ga kowa dúnia
Kowa ka bin shawa da guri sun gamu   bale fa maison dukaka nan dúnia
Ya rabbi mun roki ka tsira lakhira   ka tsarima dan bawanka ẓanba dúnia
Ka tsara uwanan har ubanan su duka   akatsar da dengimu ga ẓanba dúnia

---

36. فلولو *fululu*] from Ar. فضول "arrogant" or "exaggerated," cf. B 154; for similar interchange of ض and ل cf. line 1.

37. زكر ثى *zikir chi*] should be ذكر شى *ẓikir shi;* for meaning of *ẓikir* cf. B 88, note.

38. مومنى *mumini*] Ar. مومن *múmin* "a true believer."

امنطيو *amuntsiwa*] usually written امنشيو *amunchiwa* "confidence," from Ar. امن *áman* "to trust," with Hausa nominal suffix.

39. دوككا *dukaka*] a plural form of دوكيا *dukia* "possessions"; cf. E 35.

lit. "whoever follows lust and desire, they meet with (him)." The sense is somewhat obscure; perhaps for غموا *gamu* "meet with" we should read قموا *ḳamu* "seize upon."

C

Guard the relations of the prophet Mohammed, if they follow the law of Hin who made the world.
This song is the work of Halilu, a disciple of Shaikhu of Sanusia.
The relations of his mother all belong to his own town, the relations of hi father are men of Rima, do ye hear?
He was the son of a concubine, his mother's name was Zainabu; the nam of his father was Sidi Muktari, do ye hear?
God is the king of all, He follows them with kindness, wherefore may Shaikh of Sanusi obtain favour from Him.
O Lord, tell Sanusi that I who am here on earth, who am a child of th future world, that he may know that I ask a favour on behalf of his city
I make ready my gift for Shaikhu of Sanusi while I am on earth, Shaikh would receive anyone, much more would he receive me.
Praise be to God, we continue to render thanks before the glorious King who made the world.
After that we salute the prophet, the chosen one, the husband of Hadija, h who refused the things of the world.
To him was given everything in the world, he looked not back at it, much less did he fix his attention upon it.
It is said that stones became riches for him, for he cared not for th merchandise of earth.
He took upon himself poverty, it was better to him than wealth, that al his people might look at him, that we may follow his example.
He who follows in the way of Him who made the world, He will save him so that he shall not see pain.
With the praise of God is this song completely filled, before the gloriou God who made the world.

---

42. العم *alúma*] "relations," from Ar. عمّ *'amm*, lit. "an uncle."

44. الاهو *alaḥua*] explained by Abd-el-Kadr as "belonging to the same town." Possibly the reading should be الاهل *alaḥlu*, Ar. "members of a family."

46. For دد *dud* we should read دك *duk* "all."

شيفو *shifu*] so line 48; cf. lines 43 and 48, where it is spelt شيخ *shaikhu* Possibly *shaikhu* should be taken as a title, i.e. "Sheikh."

47. سند *sanda*] for سنسد *sanasda* "to teach."

Akatsara da alúma nabiu muhammadu   en sun bi sunna wanda yaiwo addúnia
Waka ga dan bawa halilu fa ya yita   almajirin kua shaikhu ni fa sanusia
Dengin uwa tasa du suna alahua   dengin uba nasa rimatawa kun jia
Shi dan wahaia ni uwa tasa zainabu   sunan uba nasa sidi almukhtari kun jia
Allaḥu sarki dud ya bisu da gáfara   domin fa shifu sanusi shina waiwaia
Ya rabbi sanda sanusi ni nan dúnia   dan lakhira fa shi san gari ni dogara
Na shiria kaiana ga shifu sanusi tuna na dúnia   ya doki kowa shaikhu balante nia
Alhamdu lillaḥi muna dada godia   gun jalla sarki wada yaiwo dúnia
Chuma ṣallatu ala nabiu almustsafa   gorẓo nan hadijatu wonda ya ki ta dúnia
Shi ankaba komi ga dakin dúnia   ba waiwaia ba bale shi duba ta dúnia
Anche duwatsu sun ẓamai màsa dukia   domin bukata bai kulla ba ga dúnia
Ya do talaúchi ya fiya masa dukia   don jamaa tasa aiku lura fa mu yi bia
Kowa bi suna wada yaiwo addúnia   ya tsira ba shi gani gaẓába kun jia
Tammat bihamdi allaḥi waka ta achika   gun jalla sarki wada yaiwo dúnia

---

سنوسى *sanusi*] i.e. "the founder of the city called after himself."
غرين *gari ni*] or we should perhaps read *gareni* "to me."
49. ود ييوا *wada yaiwo*] for وند ييوا *wonda ya yiwọ;* cf. line 42.
50. The first half of this line is in Arabic.
غرظ *gorẓo*] lit. "a man of strength," here apparently means "husband."
54. غذابا *gaẓába*] for عذابا *'aẓába* "pain," Ar. عذاب *'aẓáb.*
55. تمت *tammat*] from Ar. تم *tamm* "to complete."

POEM D.

D In the name of God, the Compassionate, the Merciful, may God bless our lord Mohammed and his relations and his friends, and peace be (upon them).

This is written for the instruction of my relations.

In the name of God, God is the beginning of my writing, His name is God from Him is the beginning of work.
O God, my Lord, grant us prosperity, we utter invocations, we offer supplications and prayers.
O God, creator and sustainer of thy servants, O my Lord who art worshipped and rulest over the kingdom.
O God, prepare us that we may work successfully, let us not fail or do that which is unfitting.
We will speak out, if there is anyone to listen to our words; that which you hear cast not away.
Ye too O women, my disciples, do you show diligence; invoke the name of God and offer supplications and prayers.
Put far away and leave off false dealing, leave off whispering, leave off jealousy and tale-bearing.

The author of this poem, as also of B, was a Mallam named Mohammed who lived at Birnin Gwari between Kano and Bida. It consists of: Prayer for divine assistance, 1—4; exhortation to pray and to prepare for the coming judgment, 5—9; true and false repentance, 10—12; description of the torments of hell, 13—17; exhortation to true repentance, 18—21; to prayer, 22—26; and to seek for the knowledge of God, 27—35; the journey from this world to the next, 36—38; the examination which will be held in the tomb, 39—46; general exhortations to serve God, 47—56; all shall be gathered together at the resurrection, 57—61; when the wicked shall be tormented, 62—68; and men and angels shall be judged, 69—74; prayer for salvation through Mohammed, 75—79; the necessity of making preparation for the future, 80—95; prayer for the obtaining of salvation, 96—99; ascription of praise to God, 100—101.

It should be noticed that throughout this poem ڗ *ch* is constantly substituted for ط *ts*; in the transliteration I have written *ch* throughout for the sake of uniformity. Words in this poem not found in the dictionary under ڗ *ch* should be looked for under ط *ts*.

The introductory lines are in Arabic, the word written above the line in the MS. تسليما *tasliman* "the act of saluting," is apparently intended as an emendation for سلما *salaman* "peace."

الراعت لمنسوب *alrata limansub*] this was explained by Abd-el-Kadr as "for the

POEM D.

Bismi allaḥi alrahmani alrahimi salla allaḥu ala saydina muhammadin wa áliḥi wa ṣahbiḥi wa salaman tasliman

haẓ alkitab alrata limansub

Bismi allaḥi allaḥ fárawa na ḳaratu	suna ni na allaḥ dakanan fára aiki
Ya allaḥ rabbi ka bamu gamu katerta	muna ẓikir muna addua muna ṣallati
Ya allaḥ ya khaliḳu ya arziḳi bai	ma'abudu ya rabbana sarki sarota
Ya allaḥ ka shiriamu mu yi aiki ṣawaba	kadda mu kurkura mu yi abinda ba shi kama ba
Ẓamu fa haddichi ni akan majia kalami	ba wonan da kan jishi ba shi kalkadi ba
To matamu almajiri akumaida ḥimma	kuna ẓikri kuna addua kuna ṣallati
Akuyi nesa ku ber kai da kawowa na karia	ku berta radda ku ber hasada da ananminchi

---

instruction of relations"; the words are not genuine Arabic still less Hausa. منسوب may be an incorrect derivative from Ar. نسب *nasab* "family" or "pedigree." الرعت *alrata* may possibly be from Ar. روعة *rau'at* "fear," or from Ar. رعى *ra'á* "to watch over," but the form is in either case quite irregular.

1. دكنن *dakanan*] should be دغنن *daganan* "thence."

2. كترتا *katerta*] or we should perhaps read كشرتا *kacherta* "abundance," probably from Ar. كثرة.

3. ارزق *arziḳi*] "giver of sustenance," from Ar. رزق *razaḳ*.

بى *bai*] a plural of بوا *bawa* "a slave."

معبود *ma'abudu*] Ar. "worshipped."

4. صواب *ṣawaba*] Ar. "that which is right."

كركرا *kurkura*] for كسكرا *kuskura*; lit. "to miss the mark in shooting."

5. حديث *haddichi*] cf. II. form of Ar. حدث "to explain."

6. هما *ḥimma*] cf. Ar. همّة *ḥimmat* "solicitude."

7. lit. "put far from you and give up taking away and bringing back deceitfully."

D Be afraid, there is a day of meeting between us and God; on that da whatever you are within shall be revealed.

Wherever there is any secret, any secret thieving, any envying, on that da there shall be confusion, he will say that he did it not.

My friend, repent truly and leave off falsehood, leave off deceit, leave o drinking gia and bam and buza.

Repent to God, leave off repenting like a wild cat; it repents with the fow in its mouth, it puts it not down.

He who repents like a wild cat shall indeed have nothing but evil, stripe and chains.

He shall be bound with his hands behind, he shall be dragged backward and forwards, the fire shall include everything, there shall be no end to it

He shall be dragged and beaten till the pain causes a swelling on the back in the fire is squeezing, faintness and great pain.

He cries, he gasps for breath, pain bows him down, it strikes him frequentl (as though he were) a skin (that is beaten).

Again he is taken and tied to a painful stake, he cries out, he falls dow like the beam (for pumping water).

There is indeed for ever no release at all; much less will death take hin away, so that he should go to rest.

He who repents, returns not to his work again; do you listen, we say tha there will be no giving of bribes then, though you may seek for it.

My friend, you must repent to God, you must leave off falsehood, leave of the teaching of Satan, which tends to the house of pain.

Repent truly, leave off vain deceit; if this be done, on the resurrection da your repentance will be seen.

The evil doer, if he refuses to repent, will suffer misfortune; he loses (all) he hurries himself to (the place of) pain.

Follow God, cease following the wicked man, leave both him and his desires keep the fast, and pray, and go on the pilgrimage.

---

8. ثورو *choro*] for طورو *tsoro* "fear," cf. F 6.

رنغم *rangamu*] "day of meeting with," a shortened form of رننغم *ranan gamu.*

9. جاڭكى *jachiki*] lit. "to drag the belly," an expression suggested by th crawling of a snake, applied to the secret approach of a thief.

10. غيا بم بوزا *gia bam buza*] three intoxicating drinks; *gia* is made by soak ing guinea-corn in water for three days till it begins to sprout. It is then boile and crushed and makes a highly intoxicating drink. *Bam* is palm wine obtaine by direct incision into the stem of the palm. *Buza* is made of salt, honey, an water. None of these drinks are at all commonly used in Hausaland.

11. مذورو *mazoro*] or *mazuru* "a wild cat"; the repentance of a wild cat i a Hausa synonym for insincerity; with a stolen chicken in its mouth, which i has no intention of giving up, the cat says "I repent."

Ku ji choro akoi rangamu mu da mu da allaḥ
rana na ḳomi ka ki chiki sai ta budi

Enna boiya enna jachiki enna fasada
wata rana akoi damasa ya ka che ba yi ba

Atuba haḳíḳa aboki aber na karia
aber rikichi aber sha gia da bam da buẓa

Ayi tuba ga allaḥ aber tuba maẓoro
shi ki tuba kaẓa ta tana baki bai sako ba

Maituba maẓoro ba shi ashi kowani ba
sai ẓunubi sai sanduna da su da sarka

Akandarmishi baia baia ajashi da birkido
wuta da wuta ta ki wanyi duka babu kawichi

Ajashi anadakka hal ta yin doro aẓába
chikin machichi chikin gamata chikin maṣíba

Shina kuka shina shashasha ki achiki
aẓába ana takura ana dandakasa kamal kilago

Kuma akankaishi kan rataia ga rinu aẓába
shina tsuwa shina takura kamal kutara

Shi ki nan fa daimu babu fita dadai ba
ba mutua bale shidoshi shi je shi futa

Maituba ba shi komo ga aiki nai na sabo
kun ji fa mun fadi yanda ka nemasa ba khila fa

Ayi tuba ga allaḥ aboki aber na karia
aber koiya na shaitan da ẓashi giddan aẓába

Ayi tuba haḳíḳa aber rikichi na banẓa
idan haka yi góbi anadubu nadama

Maiṣuabo iẓan ya ki tuba ya yi khasára
ya rubushi ya kora kansa chikin aẓába

Ku bi allaḥ ku ber bi läinu da shi da nafsi
kuna aẓumi da ṣalla kuna zaka da haji

---

13. lit. "he has been bound behind behind, he is dragged away and comes again; fire and fire end everything, there is no edge."

14. غاماتا *gamata*] cf. Ar. غمى *gamá* "a fainting fit."

15. تكرا *takura*] lit. "causes him to coil up like a snake."

16. رن *rinu*] properly an iron fork for toasting meat.

كتارا *kutara*] is the long cross beam which acts as a lever for drawing water from a well.

20. نداما *nadama*] Ar. ندامة *nadámat* "repentance."

22. لعين *läinu*] Ar. *la'in* "accursed."

D Leave off saying your prayers late, make your prayers at the right time; he who without cause is late in saying his prayers shall have no success.
He who refuses to pray is indeed a heathen; he will not be able to resist at the last day he will see the abode of pain.
Leave off consulting even a little as to what you should do; take to yourselves diligence, every man shall receive his measure (of reward).
Sleep and awake, rise up and show diligence; pray and offer up praise and supplication.
Sleep not the sleep of the ignorant and careless; he stretches his limbs, he rolls like an ant.
Till the sun comes forth he remains in his house and comes not out, his wits remain at home.
The son of the wicked man is the friend of the heathen, the brother of the Jew; leave them alone, the day is coming when they will meet with God.
We tell and warn you, my friends; love God, love the prophet, love friendship.
We cause you to hear of friendship, it comes not to this earth for ever cleave to it, continue to incline your ears to it.
Give attention, that I may explain to you the truth which I have; let not your ears be stubborn like those of a profligate man.
If you have children seek instruction for them, take them to the Mallams that they may learn by heart.
Follow after God, prostrate yourself before Him, pray and obtain pardon, pray yet again.
Leave off pride, gain much instruction; God will increase the prosperity of him who is instructed.
Leave off hastening after the things of this world and to prepare for it, rise up, O my relations, for we have a journey before us.
That journey which you take is to the city of the servants (of God); keep knowledge, you know the precepts of God.
I do not fear death or burial; you are journeying to a strange city to which thou hast never before come.

---

23. تكوقتتا *taka wakatita*] a better reading probably is تعوقتتا *ta a wakatita*, cf. MS.

24. غرى *gari*] for غريش *gareshi* "to him."

25. سوف سوف *sofa sofa*] this is apparently an Arabic particle indicating the future.

28. برزا *birza*] lit. "the mud out of which the wall is built," here equivalent to "within the house."

29. The first syllable دى *di* of the second half of this line is part of the last word in the first half, cf. lines 33, 43, 69. This is unusual, as the sense usually breaks off at the end of the first half.

Ku ber makara da ṣalla ku yi taka waḳatita   maimakara da ganga ba ayi masa arziki ba
Kowa ya ki ṣalla ko tabetta kafiri ni   ba makawa gari góbi ya ga giddan aẓába
Ku ber bi shawora sofa sofa da sanu na yi   ku do aníya kowa shi samu gulgudusa
Ku yi berchi ku falaka ku tashi ku maida ḥimma   kuna ṣalla kuna tasbaha kuna ṣallati
Kadda ka yi kwanchi jáḥili da ba shi kulla ba   shina mika shina birkima kaman da chocha
Hal rana ta fudu shina daki bai fito ba   idan ya fita hankalinsa shi fa da birẓa
Da mazugu aboki majusi kani yahu-   -di abersu kuru akoi rangamasu da su da allaḥ
Muna waátsi muna galḳadi gareku dengi   aso allaḥ aso anabi aso ẓumunchi
Mu yi ku ji ẓumunta ba shi je abada kasa ba   anatsaushi ku kuna dada karkattawa
Ku karḳatta ḳunua en gaia maku gaṣkiana   kadda ku chaia da kuni kaman kuni asheggi
En kun samu yaya ku nema laddabi gar-   -esu ku kaisu ga mallamasu shinni su samu harda
Ku bi allaḥ kuna sajada kuna roko   kuna roḳo ku sa gáfara ku ka ka ruanka
Ku ber fahari ku yi laddabi da girma   mailaddabi allaḥ shi kan safa arziḳisa
Ku ber garaji ẓama dúnia da shiriwa   ku yi tashi dengi akoi taffía gabbanmu
Taffía chan da kuna ẓo gari gabawa   ku rika shinni kuna sani sunna ga allaḥ
Ba mutua ni ki razána ba zaman kushiwa   ku yi taffían bako gari ba ka tso dadai ba

---

31. The text in this line is probably corrupt.

34. The meaning is somewhat obscure, and the text probably corrupt. According to Abd-el-Kadr for *ka ka ruanka* we should read قارا روقو *ḳara roḳo*, "increase your prayers"; the letter ع at the end of the first half of the line is apparently superfluous.

س *sa*] a shortened form of سم *sama* "to obtain."

37. غرى غباوا *gari gabawa*] lit. "the city for the slave," i.e. the city of the servants of God; or we might perhaps read *gabbawa*, taking this as a lengthened form of *gabba* "ahead."

38. ظوا *tso*] for ذوا *ẓo* "to come."

D If thou art brought and laid in the grave, there will be no one there but thine own self.

If you have done good you will come to a wide place; if thou hast done evil thou wilt meet with great pain.

And the angel Nakir will come to question thee, and with him Mankaru with club and whip and strong sticks.

If they come across a man who has served a vain service, who has worshipped a stone, who has made the stump of a tree (his god),

He begins to tremble as he sees them, he begins to be afraid; when they ask him, he has no reason or answer to give.

They pile up blows many in number as little stones, they give blows three at a time.

If they come across a man who understands the greatness of (God) the King, if they question him but he has no reason or answer to give,

They give a reason and answer to him who trembles; they look in his face, they know that he is a believer.

O my relations, we direct you unto Mohammed; we all seek the knowledge of God that we may not fail in speech.

O God my Lord, do thou help us that I may feel happy; he who is in the shade knows not what is done outside.

You will be sought for and found in the next world, when all people are gathered together; no skill or craft will by any means (avail).

Let us take care, let us follow the path of those who are guided; let us not desert it, Satan leads us by a black way.

Ye too, O women my disciples, do you show diligence and take pains, do you serve God,

Say your full prayers, fulfil the fast; be not stubborn nor walk proudly, your husband is to you as a Mallam.

---

39. كاشى *kasshi*] "to continue" as in B 54; or we should perhaps read *ka isshi* "thou meetest with."

سى حلنكا *sai hallinka*] lit. "but thine own character."

41. According to Mohammedan tradition soon after a corpse is laid on the tomb two black angels named Monker and Nakir come to hold an examination into the faith of the deceased man. If he answer rightly his body is left to rest in peace till the resurrection, if otherwise he is beaten till he roars so loud as to be heard by all from east to west except men and genii. The body is then guarded by ninety-nine dragons till the resurrection.

42. باوا *bawa*] lit. "a slave," an expression used of men generally as being the slaves of God, cf. δοῦλοι Θεοῦ in N.T.

43. ذوروا اكل *ẓoro akal*] for طوروا اكن *tsoro akan*.

44. مى مى *mai mai*] for مينى مينى *mainya mainya* "very many."

بكتا *bukata*] should probably be بغتا *bugata* "blows."

En akaika anshifi da ka chikin kushiwa   ba kasshi kowonı chikinta sai hallinka
En akanaiku khaira kun tso ku iski yelwa   en shara ka aika ka tso ka sha maṣíba
Wa nakiri shi ẓo tanbaiaka da shi da   munkaru da gudumai da kurafu da sanduna na karifi
Iẓan iski bawa wanda ki bauta ta banẓa   shina bauta ga duchi shina yi gatsana itachi
Shi dora makarkata ya ganesu shi dora ẓo-   -ro akal suka tabaies ba shi huja ba ko shi amsa
Su kan ribi sanduna mai mai kaman duachu   su dora bukata suna sa masu uku uku
Iẓa(n) iski bawa wonda ya san jalla sarki   iẓan suka tabi ba shi huja ko shi amsa
Su kan kawa dalíli da huja maikatarta   su ka doro suka bershi suna so mumini ni
To ku näifi mu yi shiri tun ga ahmadu   dúnia mu nemi shinni don kadda mu kasa fadi jawabi
Allaḫ ubangíji ka ka tarshimu ji dadi   shina ennua bai san abinda akayi wari ba
Akanbidi samaku a lakhira dúnia atarat   babu chimi ankuma kuma ba dabára
Mu do (a)nía muna bi tafar ka masushirya   kadda mu saki shaitsa(n) shi kaimu bakin tafarki
To matamu almajirai akumaida ḫimma   ku do anía kuna ḳokari kuna ibáda
Kuna ṣalla chikaka kuna aẓumi chikaka   kadda ku chaia kuna takama almanjinka mallama

---

45. تبى *tabi*] a shortened form of تمبى *tambaia* "to question."

46. س *so*] according to Abd-el-Kadr we should read سنى *sani* "know."

47. Text and meaning obscure. If the transliteration given above be correct *näifi* is equivalent to *dengi* "relations"; we should perhaps read *tukuna* "not yet," or "yet awhile."

شرى *shiri*] may be for *shiria* "guidance," cf. line 50; or for *shiru* "silence"; if the latter be the correct reading, translate "we keep silence yet awhile in regard to Mohammed."

دنيا *dúnia*] according to Abd-el-Kadr is equivalent to *duka* "all."

48. ورى *wari*] probably from Ar. ورا *wará* "beyond," or "on the other side."

49. سمكو *samaku*] "to find you," or we should perhaps read *samàko* "to arrive early."

50. دو نيا *do nía*] shortened form of *doka anía* "take care," cf. following line.

52. المنجنك *almanjinka*] for المجنك *almijinka* "thy husband.

D You my children, my disciples, do you show diligence, do you seek after th knowledge of God; be strenuous, ye are the heirs of the Mallams.

Seek after true and correct knowledge, leave off changing; be not stubbor nor walk proudly, your father is to you as a Mallam.

The children of the prophets and the wives of the prophe sought aft knowledge, they were diligent, they served God.

Much more do you, O mothers of these children, take care lest your relatio leave you outside (heaven).

Very many shall come together, there shall be much to eat, do ye hear; h who is late shall have nothing but muddy water to drink.

Behind will be terror, in front of us will be the city of the resurrection; w shall all be gathered together, even to our ancestor Adam.

And the angels and genii shall be gathered together and shall surround us myriads and myriads of them shall be collected, judgment shall b prepared.

Line after line shall be raised up there at the resurrection, that space of th Bait al Mukaddas shall be sufficient for us.

On that day when we have been gathered together and restored to life, division shall be made, the wicked shall be left to suffer trouble.

On that day you shall speedily obtain heaven; others (will say) Would that had known; they will feel remorse.

On that day the secret place shall be laid open; in the midst of the assembl every one shall know thee and thy character.

The (heat of) the sun shall descend (increased) seventy-thousand-fold; its hea shall wither up our arms and the heat of its orb shall (burn) our heads.

It will continually blister our heads, it will soften them; the skull will bo over as a cooking vessel does.

On that day a little drinking-water shall be sought for, there shall be n limit to the great heat, there shall be thirst and pain.

Thirst shall burn the tongue down to the throat, it shall burn the spleen, th liver, the heart and the parts below.

---

56. Or "much more do ye, O children of our wives."

57. اكن غد ترى *akanguda tari*] for *akantari guda* "many shall be gathere together." *guda* is a word usually prefixed to numerals, its meaning being somewh the same as the English expression "in number." Thus *guda uku* "three in number or occasionally "three times." Possibly the reading here should be كى غد ترى *akoi guda tari*, cf. MS.

59. الجنّ *aljinnu*] Ar. جنّ *jinn*. Invisible beings intermediate between me and angels or devils.

60. عثم *acham*] for عثن *achan* or better, اثن *achan*.

Ku yayamu almajirai akumaida ḥimma
ku nema shinni kuna kokari da ku gaji mallama

Ku nema shinni haḳíḳa da gaṣḳia ku ber saḳi-
-wa kadda ku chaia kuna takamal ubaka mallama

Yayan anabawa da matamu anabawa
su nema shinni suna kokari suna ibáda

Bali ku fa matamu yaya nana
ku do anía ḳadda yan uwanku su berku ha(in)ya

Akanguda tari ni da anchia tari kú ji
maimákara ba shi sha rua ba sai na guiba

Baia rázani na gabbanmu gari ḳiama
akantarshimu dukamu hal kakanmu adamu

Da malaiku da aljinnu su tari su kewoiyimu
ribbi da ribbi antaru ẓaashiri hukumchi

Akan ṣaffu ṣaffu ayatada acham ḳiáma
sarari na bait almuḳaddas ta ishimu

Rana chan akantataramu araiyimu
akan ẓabi aber guriguri suna mayata

Rana na da manmaẓa kun samu girma
wansu suna da na sani suna nidama

Rana chan akuntuna loloki asiri
chaka jamaa kowa shi sanka shi sa(n) halinka

Akan safko da rana ribbi sabäin
chakani asanya chikai chakani gudanta du ḳawanamu

Ta kan rika farcha kai garemu ta ẓabki
ḳolua tana tafassa tana habuma kaman tuḳúnia

Rana na akannemi guwa baiyaka
zafi yaiyawa ga kishirua ga chananta

Kishirua che akansurya halshi hal
makurua ta so(i)ya sefa da anta da ẓuchia da saifa

بيت المقدس *bait almuḳaddas*] Ar. "the sacred house"; probably refers to the Kaaba at Mecca, though the same expression is often used of Jerusalem.

62. منمذا *manmaẓa*] or *maimaẓa*, cf. MS. for *maẓa maẓa* "very quickly."

دا نا سني *da na sani*] lit. "that which I knew." According to Abd-el-Kadr this is equivalent to the Ar. ليت *laita* "would that!"

64. سفكو *safko*] for سبكو *sabko*, usually pronounced *sapko*.

ثكاني *chakani*] should be *ẓakani*, cf. Ar. ذكا *ẓaká* "to blaze."

65. فرشي *farcha*] for فرسي *farsa* "to blister."

66. ثننتا *chananta*] for طننتا *tsananta*.

D There shall be heat of perspiring, heat of the sun, heat of many; there sha be no shade except where the shelter of Mohammed is.
There are seven, each of which is set up; beneath each you see the faithfu (gathered).
He whose wishes God gratifies, feels happy; he has shade, he knows no what is without.
Hell shall come in hope that men may be left to fall therein; it will gaz with open mouth in hope that a multitude may be given (to it).
Seventy thousand evil angels shall be put therein, the fire will roar and mak a noise, like the splitting of wood,
Until God hath finished His judgment on His servants; some shall be carrie to heaven, some to hell.
May God preserve us safely that we may be saved, among all those who ar on the right hand of Mohammed.
We shall enjoy shelter, we shall drink water in the wide plain; we shal have pleasure, being gathered together in the presence of Mohammed.
We shall be brought to the pond of the prophet; we shall drink and wash and rise up and walk, and hasten to our homes.
We the servants of God shall enter heaven, the dwelling-place of the father of Abraham; houses shall be given to each one of us, each shall go to his own farm.
There shall be pleasure of every varying kind; we shall be saved in heaven for the sake of Mohammed.
To the house of safety, the house of constant abode, the house of happiness the heavenly house, in which to remain, may God bring us.
O my brothers, to you do we speak in order that you may make preparation; you know that the Lord is not unjust to his servants.
If you follow Him and revere Him, He will grant you salvation; if you do evil, He will bring you to the abode of pain.
He made the abode of fire, He left it for the sake of evil doers; there are seven divisions in it, its depth exceeds all comparison.

---

68. رانا *rana*] according to Mohammedan tradition the sun will at this time approach within a mile of the earth.

غا ترتى *ga tariti*] meaning obscure—perhaps we should read غا تر نى *ga tara ni* "behold the crowd."

71. تفا *ta fa*] according to Abd-el-Kadr we should read تفاد *ta fada*.

72. زبانيا *zabánia*] explained by Abd-el-Kadr as "evil angels." الزبانية *az-zabániyat* occurs once in the Koran, c. 96, v. 18, where its meaning is very uncertain. It is not a genuine Arabic word.

رور بيكى ثثاغى *ruri baiki chachagi*] *ruri* is used of the bellowing of an ox, *baiki* or better *babaki* of the groaning of a camel, and *chachagi* of the crackling of split wood or torn paper.

Ga koni jibbi ga ta rana ga tariti   ba ennua sai enda tuti muhammad
Tuta che guda tokkos kowa che ankafa-   -ta kowa ka ga kalkashita mumina
Wanda ubangíji ya katarsasa ya ji dadi   shina ennua bai san abinda akayi wari ba
Jaḥannama kan taffo wai aberta ta fa   taro ta gano bakinta na saki wai abata
Asanya zabánia wa dubu sabäin chakani   tana ruri tana baiki kamal chachagi
Hal allaḥ shi wanya hukumchi nai ga bayi   wadansu akaisu aljenna wadansu akai jaḥannama
Ya allaḥ shi samu chiraro mu chira   chakan jemaa wananda kan dama che muhammad
Mu sha ennua mu sha kauchara chikin baiala   mu sha nima antataramu gabban muhammad
Akaimu kundumi ya rasulu mu sha mu wa-   -nka mu taka tadowa muna hamzari ẓua giddanmu
Mu je aljenna baia gidda nana hubal khalílu   abamu giddadaji kowanimu shi je gonasa
En nima da launi kaman(u) bam da banbam   antarshimu aljennati midon muhammad
Giddan chira giddan dawama giddan sa'ada   giddan aljenna giddan tabetta allaḥ shi kaimu
To kua yan uwa muna gaia maku don ku shiria   ku san fa ubangíji ba shi tsulumi che ga bawa
En ka bishi ka charkakashi (shi) baka chira   en ṣuabo ka kan yi shi kaika giddan aẓába
Ya giddan wuta ya beri don masuṣuabo   rabunta bokkoi zurfinta ya fi gabban michali

---

76. كندمى *kundumi*] i.e. the pond of Mohammed just outside paradise, believed to be a month's journey in circumference and to have as many drinking cups set round it as there are stars in the sky.

77. حبل خليل *hubal khalílu*] should be *ubal halílu*, cf. MS. *khalílu* Ar. lit. "friend" is the usual title of Abraham.

غددجى *giddadaji*] for *giddaji*, pl. of *gidda* "a horse."

78. مدن *midon*] should be دمن *domin* "because of."

79. سعادا *sa'ada*] from Ar. سعادة *sa'ádat* "happiness."

82. These seven divisions of hell will be assigned respectively to wicked Mohammedans, Jews, Christians, Sabians, Magians, idolaters and hypocrites, the punishment in each being worse than in the one above it.

D We prepare you, O my relations, for work which will bring prosperity; it is not in order that you may give us anything to eat that we instruct you.
The love of God and of the prophet will be with us; we follow them in this world until all shall love them, until such love shall be permanently established.
This earth is an abode of gossip, an abode which passes away; an abode of deceit, an abode of poverty, an abode which comes to an end.
He makes preparation that he may remain and continue in this world; this desire is indeed a foolish one.
If thou talkest much, my words to restrain you are ended; death is coming it will prevent you from heaping up words.
Thou wilt leave behind the dwellings of earth, thou wilt not take them with thee; thou wilt only have a shroud and a shirt.
You will come to a place where you know no skill (that will avail), still less any contrivance; there will be no guidance for you on that day, still less preparation.
Alas such an one had not the sense to consider; he did nothing remarkable his sense was as that of a fool.
He whom the Lord fills with His wisdom so that he keeps a careful look out until evening is prosperous.
He who is very thirsty takes pains to dig a well; beware lest death take him away to a place where he will do no work.
He who would repent let him take pains to repent (now); beware lest the door be closed and he who is outside should not be able to enter in.
We indeed speak a little as it were in parables, we do not make exact distinctions; we keep silent, understanding is the measure of all things.
For that which is true hath been understood and explained, will keep silence, there is no knowledge with him, still less......
May God deliver us and save us with an excellent salvation; (He who is) the father of Abraham, Who was in the beginning and will continue for ever.

---

83. بكى *buki*] properly a marriage-feast.

84. اسنت *asanta*] we should probably read *asonta* "loved"; the construction of the line is very uncertain.

85. كانكا *kanika*] according to Abd-el-Kadr this should be *kankani*, which is probably equivalent to *kankanchi*.

87. فوا *fua*] should probably be قوا *ḳua* "also."

88. حوسك *hausaki*] should be عوسغى *'ausagi* "a shirt put on under the shroud."

Muna shiri ku dengi ga aiki maikaterta	muna foronku ba don ku ᐧ bamu abin buki ba
Mu kamna allaḥ da anabi ta ishimu	bi nan dúnia ḥal asanta ḥal ya chawanta
Giddan dúnia giddan kanika giddan maiata	giddan rudi gidda anmacha giddan kári
Ya yi tatali don shi girku shi ẓamna dúnia	so wanda so wanda ba shi hankali ba
Iẓan ka tanka fadawa hannamaka su kaka-	-ri ajali ka taho fua hannamaku taru-ansu
Ka kan ber tarikachi dúnia ba ka tso da su ba	sai kafan da hausaki akan gareka
Ku kan taffi dam ba ka san chima bali dabára	babu shiriya ra na gareka bali ku shirya
Kaicho wanan na yi hanḳali ba shi duba	ba ba shina lajabi shi hanḳali(n)sa badan badada
Wanda ubangíji ya chika masa hanka-linsa	shi kan gani kami marechi arziḳi ni
Kowa ya iẓanwa shi do (a)nía shi yasa	kadda mutua fa dokeshi hal ila ya baia
Kowa kan tuba shi do anía shi tuba	kadda arufi kofa shina wakan ya shifo ba
Mu dai mu yi machali kadan ba mu rarafiya	muna kurum hankali duka shi kiyasi
Don wota gaṣḳia akansanta akanwaiita	na yi kurum ba shinni biḥi bali akanyi
Ya allaḥ shi samu chira acheto fiyayi	saidafari maiyo da góbi hubal khalílu

---

92. بيا *baia*] equivalent to *ba ya yi.*

93. وكن يسيفو *wakan ya shifo*] the true reading (according to Abd-el-Kadr) is وجى بيشغو *woji ba ya shiggo.*

94. ررفعايا *rarafiya*] according to Abd-el-Kadr this should be رربيبا *rarabai ba*, *rarabi* being an intensive form of *raba* "to divide."

95. به *biḥi*] Ar. "with him"; in the latter part of this line the text is corrupt.

96. حبل *hubal*] for عبل *ubal* or *uban*, cf. line 77, note.

سيدفرى *saidafari*] probably intended for ميدفرى *maidafari* "He who was in the beginning."

D Father of Kasim, father of Tsahiru and of Tsibi, father of Rakia and Fatim and of the mother of Kulthum.

The blessing of God (be upon him), may God increase love and salvation, an faith and trust in our lord Mohammed.

God is our salvation, and he who seeks for the truth will continue with th friends and relations of Mohammed.

100 Say, Thanks be to God, we seek the praise of God; we give thanks an are grateful to God.

Say, Thanks be to God, we seek the praise of Mohammed; we give thank and are grateful on account of Mohammed.

Praise be to God, the Lord of the worlds, blessing and peace be upon th messenger of God. May God bless him and give him peace. It i ended. Amen.

We love God; may He grant to us the obtaining of prosperity.

O thou who lookest on the writing, ask pardon for the scribe thereof, haply the scribe thereof may escape from hell-fire.

We invoke the name of God, we offer prayer and supplication.

---

97. The first three (according to Abd-el-Kadr) were sons, the last three wer daughters, of Mohammed. For Rakia we should read Rukaiya. Cf. B 21, note.

ادم *adum*] should be دام *da um* "and the mother," cf. B 21, note.

The writing enclosed within the curve of the illustration is in Arabic, als the four lines in the centre below, the same two lines being repeated. Th

Uban ḳasim uban tsaḥiri da su da tsibi   uban raḳia uban fatsimat adum kultum
Ṣalla allaḥ allaḥ shina dada so da chira   da aminchi da yir(d)a ga sidina muhammad
Chira ma namu allaḥ da ya shi nima aminchi   shina tabetta gun ṣahba da wa alwali muhammad
Afada alhamdu allaḥi mu nemi yabo ga allaḥ   muna shukra muna godia ẓua ga allaḥ
Afada alhamdu allaḥi mu nemi yabo muhammad   muna shukra muna godia don muhammad

al-hamdu li-lláḥi rabbi-l-'álamína aṣ-ṣalát wa-ssalám 'alá rasúli-lláḥi ṣalla-lláḥ 'alaihi wa sallama tammat amin

muna kamna allaḥ shi bamu gamuwa katerta
ya nádzira-l-khaṭṭi istagfir likátibihi
la'alla kátibaḥu yanjú mina-n-nárí
muna ẓikri muna addua muna ṣallati

Arabic below should be written thus:

يا ناظر الخط استغفر لكاتبه
لعل كاتبه ينجوا من النار

These two lines are written in the Basît (بسيط) metre, which is as follows:

⏓⏓ | ⏑– | ⏓⏑– || ⏓⏓ | ⏑– | ⏓⏓– |

It is one of the most commonly used in modern Arabic poetry.

POEM E.

E In the name of God, the Compassionate, the Merciful; may the peace of God
be upon him, after whom there is no prophet.
We thank the Lord, the ruler of the kingdom, who has sent Mohammed
son of Amina.
We pour forth salutations on account of his excellency, and the relations of
Mohammed who excels all.
Listen, O companions of Abd-el-Kadr; our (evil) deeds shall be reckoned unless
we repent.
He who is ungrateful shall not be saved; let us repent, let us put away
ingratitude, so that we may be saved.
Leave off imitating the worship of the heathen, see what Yinfa did and he
was driven away.
When we come to the war and conquer the heathen, their goods shall be
gathered together and the price fixed.
When the reckoning is made a division will take place, the share assigned
to a horse and its owner will be put out.
And each soldier when he comes receives a share; let us repent of carrying
off booty secretly, lest we burn in the fire.
Both the judge and those who come to receive judgment (shall burn)
repent, leave off following the desire of your heart.

The author of this poem and of F was Sheikh Othman, who died in 1809. The name of the copyist was Ramalan son of Yusuf. Its object was to rouse the people to take part in the war which he was just commencing against the Hausas, Othman being himself a Fulah. The final result of this war was the conquest by Othman of the greater part of the Hausa States and their nominal acceptance of the Mohammedan faith. The poem also contains an appeal to join in the pilgrimage to Mecca.

It consists of: Introduction, 1—3; exhortation to repent and to give up idolatry, 4—6; the spoils in the coming war shall be fairly divided, 7—9; the judgment of God is to be feared, 10—12; need of liberality, of purity of life and of repentance in view of the war and of the judgment to come, 13—28; exhortation to join in the pilgrimage to Mecca, 29—38; the route to be followed, 39—48; prayers and praises to be offered at Mecca, 49—52.

Throughout this poem is to be noted the Sokoto custom of using ش *shi* for ژ *chi*. Cf. lines 7. 10. 12. etc.

POEM E.

Bismi allaḥi errahmáni errahími   ṣalla allaḥu ala man la nabiyi ba'daḥu
Mu godi ubangíji sarki sarota   da ya aiko muhamadu dan amina
Muna ẓuba eṣṣallati bisa. fiyaiyi   da umatan muhamadu ya fi kowa
Ku sorara jama'a alḳadirawa   hallinmu da ankaẓana sai mu tuba
Da ya shi maibutulshi ba shi tsira   mu tuba mu ber butulshi ko mu tsira
Ku ber sun maida addini na asna   abin ga da yinfa ya yi ankakosai
Iẓan mun ẓo jaḥádi mu shi asna   agangama dukiansu akawamata
Iẓan ankawamata ararabata   rabon doki da maidoki afisai
Wa dakara randa ya ẓo du ya samu   mu tuba da shin gululu kadda mu kona
Da alkaḷi da masuẓua sheria   ku tuba ku ber bian son ẓushia ba

---

3. عمات *umata*] "relations," cf. C 42, note.

4. القادراوا *alḳadirawa*] Abd-el-Kadr was Othman's principal Mallam and a native of Kano; *alḳadirawa* is therefore probably equivalent to "people of Kano." Cf. F 5.

6. ينف *yinfa*] Yinfa was a king of Gober; he seized and sold a number of men from Sokoto but was shortly afterwards overcome.

7. شى *shi*] a Sokoto use for ثى *chi* "take possession of," cf. *shin* for *chin* line 9.

اكوماتا *akawamata*] cf. Ar. قوّم *ḳawwama* "to estimate price of."

8. افسى *afisai*] for افتسدش *afitasdashi* "there shall be put out."

9. غلول *gululu*] cf. Ar. غلّ *galla* "to embezzle." Cf. F 204.

10. ذشيا *ẓushia*] for ذثيا *ẓuchia* "heart."

E If thou regardest the text, understand it well, and its explanation; regard the two commentaries thereon.

If judgment be given we shall all receive (our deserts); let us fear the meeting with Him who has power over all.

If the standards of war be unfolded, let us come and go forth with our goods and our wives.

(If any of you) stay at home, staying of necessity, if you have provisions give to those (who fight); you will receive a reward.

You who steal the earnest money (will be punished) unless you repent; deceit is the kingdom of the heathen.

Leave off playing darra and deceit, O Mussulmans; leave off drumming and going about with bad women.

Those who go to sit in the place of intoxication behold that which is unlawful they refuse to repent.

Those of you who continue in the ways of Mussulmans, repent, leave off discord lest you come to the fire.

Those who frequent the gates of the cities pay all their attention to women.

Repent, leave off this; we know that if any of you refuse to repent ye shall all burn in the fire.

And (concerning) evil living without marriage, (God) shall cause those (who live thus) to be blotted out.

And those of you who seek for adornment in order that they may be seen shall be punished, all of you (who) refuse to repent.

He who refuses to follow the instruction of our fathers will share in the abode of those who are in the fire.

Repent, give up refusing, listen, cease to be jealous of us and to whisper evil and speak lies.

(Leave off) pride and evil-doing, and stealing earnest money; count thy cowries full, leave off falsehood.

---

11. نص *naṣṣi*] Ar. نصّ *naṣṣ*, used of the text of the Koran.

ذيى *ẓiaya*] for جيى *jiaya*, a lengthened form of جى *ji* "to understand," cf. line 20.

شرحوحى *sharhohi*] "commentaries," cf. Ar. شرح *sharh* "commentary."

حلل ثانى *halil chani*] explained by Abd-el-Kadr as the names of two commentaries on the Koran, which he said were written 720 years ago. Possibly for حلل *halil* we should read جلال *jalál*, and ثانى may be Ar. for "second." There were two commentators both named Jelálu-d-dín, one of whom died 1459 A.D. the other 1505 A.D.

14. ضرور *ḍarura*] cf. Ar. ضرور "necessity" or "compulsion."

15. تبن امان *tabin amana*] in Kano this would be تسن امان *chin amana*

Iẓan ku dubi naṣṣi ku yi ẓiaya   da sharhohi ku dubi halil da chani
Iẓan ankai hukumshi du mu karba   mu tsarshi gamu da maiikò da kowa
Iẓan anfida tutoshi jahádi   mu zo mu da dukia mu taffi da mata
Ẓama kasan ẓama domin ḷarura   akoi gúẓuri ku basu ku samu lada
Da masutabin amana sai ku tuba   da tsalumshi sarota nan ta asna
Ku ber na darra da tsalumshi musulmi   kidda molo ku ber yawo da karma
Da masuẓua mashaya don su ẓamna   suna dubi haramu sun ki tuba
Da masuẓama ga ha(i)nyoyi musulmi   ku tuba ku ber fasadi kadda ku kona
Da masuẓua ga kofofin birani   su tatara hankalinsu zua ga mata
Ku tuba ku ber abin nana mu yi ẓiaya   iẓan kowa kun ki tuba du ku kona
Da fasishiwan ẓina babu amri   da ya sa ankashashafi wadansu
Da masubida wushiwa don asansu   anaforonku kulun kun ki tuba
Da wanda fa ya ki bin foron ubamu   su tara gidda da su da wutan jahíma
Ku tuba ku ber kiyaya ku yi ẓiaya   ku ber muna hasada da radda da karia
Da girmankai da zanba da shin amana   ku zama shika alkawara ku ber na karia

---

cf. line 25, "to steal the earnest money paid by a buyer as a preliminary to purchase."

16. در *darra*] a game played with stones or cowries, which are placed in small holes in a square marked out on the ground. It is generally considered as a disreputable game.

كرما *karma*] for كروا *karua* "a prostitute."

17. مشايا *mashaya*] explained by Abd-el-Kadr as *wurin shan gia* "the place where intoxicating liquor is drunk."

19. تتر حنكلنس *tatara hankalinsu*] lit. "they gather together their wits." For use of *tatara* cf. D 61.

22. وشيوا *wushiwa*] probably from Ar. وشى *washyun* "adornment."

23. تار غدا *tara gidda*] lit. "to share a house with."

E The Mussulman who loves his brother shall share the abode of Mohammed son of Amina.
Pay attention and listen to my words, O Mussulmans; that which has been said is true.
If then you refuse to repent (or) even to listen, when you have to rise (and leave this world) there will be no continuance for anyone.
If the king of the Mussulmans goes to Mecca, we must pray, and make ready our goods (to go with him).
Our belief is to us in the place of riches; we cleanse our hearts, we repent well.
We pray that our Lord may give us power, that we may rise up amongst all the followers of Abd-el-Kadr.
Ye who are good and faithful, rise up, we pray that our Lord may take us with you.
Ye hypocrites and heathen stay (where you are); leave off rejoicing, the fire will devour you later on.
We pray to the Lord, the ruler of the kingdom, if we start, that we may obtain provision for our journey from the heathen.
With our wives, our children, all our slaves and our goods, we Mussulmans will go together.
And our blind and halt and aged, and whoever is afraid, we will all go together.
We will travel too without thirst or hunger; we will rejoice in that which is sweet one with another.
By the power of God, and the blessing of our friend, He will bring us to the place where a share shall be granted to all.
When we have prepared our goods and have started, from Tumba we follow the road to Bakura.
When we start from the town of Bakura, we come to the town of Talata, we sleep there.
When we start from the town of Talata, we follow the road to Jata, we sleep there.
When we start from there we give diligence to reach Danisa and sleep at Bungudu.

---

27. ذى *zi*] for جى *ji* "listen to." Cf. line 11.

من *muna*] for *mana* "then" or "indeed," so line 24 etc.

29. سركى مسلمى *sarki musulmi*] "king of the Mussulmans." This is the title usually given to the Sultan of Sokoto.

30. ايمنش *aimanshi*] for ايمنث *aimanchi*, from Ar. ايمان *ímán* "faith" with Hausa nominal suffix.

راكم *rakumi*] "camels," used here in the sense of wealth.

Musulmi wanda ya so dan uwa tai   su tara gidda da ahmada dan amina
Ku sorara ku ẓi magana musulmi   abinda akayi fada muna gaskia na
Iẓan dai kun ki tuba ai ẓiaya   iẓan ya tashi babu ẓama ga kowa
Iẓan sarki musulmi ẓashi makka   akayi muna addua amushiria kaya
Fa aimanshimu a rakuminmu   mu tsarkaka ẓushianmu mu kiota tuba
Mu roki ubangíẓinmu shi bamu iko   mu tashi shikin jamaʻa alḳadirawa
Da ṣalihai da muminai ku tashi   mu roki ubangíẓinmu shi kaimu tari
Munafikai da kafirai ku ẓamna   ku ber murna wuta atashiku baia
Mu roki ubangízi sarki sarota   iẓan muna tashi mu yi gúẓuri da asna
Da matanmu da yayanmu da bai du   da dukoki musulmi ẓamu tari
Makafinmu guragunmu da tsofi   wani kaki ẓulumi duka ẓamu tari
Mu kua taffi babu kishirua babu yunwa   shikin dadi muna murna da juna
Da yi allaḥ da albarkar waliya   ya kaimu gari da ankaraba da ḳowa
Iẓan mu shiria kaia munka tashi   ta tunba mu ki biawa har bakura
Iẓan mu tashi da birnin bakura   mu ẓo birnin talata nan mu kwana
Iẓan mu tashi da birnin talata   ta jata mu ki biawa nan mu kwana
Iẓan mu tashi da nan mun yi hinma   ta danisa da bungudu ẓamu kwana

---

33. منافكى *munafikai*] "hypocrites," cf. Ar. منافق *munáfiḳ* "hypocrite."
اتشيك *atashiku*] equivalent to ذاتشيك *ẓatachiku* "shall devour you."
38. د يى *da yi*] a Sokoto expression for دايكون *da ikọn* "by the power of."
وليى *waliya*] "friend," i.e. Mohammed.
39. تتنب *ta tunba*] "of Tunba," understand *hainya* "road."
42. حنم *hinma*] for حمّ *himma* "diligence," cf. following line, probably from Ar. همّة *ḥimmat* "eagerness."

E When we start from here we travel diligently, we come to Kutarkushi, w put down our baggage.
When we come to Kutarkushi, we start and turn aside from the road t Zaria, we leave it on the right.
We turn aside from Kano and Bauchi, we leave them on the left; we com to Kurarafa, we put down our goods.
When we start from here we travel diligently, we come to Madangana, th river of Wakari.
When we start from here we travel diligently, we follow it, we travel eas as far as Adamawa.
When we start from Adamawa we come to the country of Bagu, we pu down our goods.
May (God) bring us to the city without lack of anything; with joy we shal meet with the Arabs.
When we come to Mina we rest there; we go to Mecca and pass it to go t Medina.
We pour forth salutations on Mohammed, and on the relations of Mohammed who surpasses all,
And on his friends, and the followers of his followers; we offer prayers, ma we obtain salvation.

The writing of this journey is finished; the name of the copyist i Ramalan son of Yusuf; praise be to God and good success and salutations an peace to the messenger of God.

---

47. حى *hai*] for حر *har* "until," so in line 50.

50. منار *munar*] i.e. Wady Mina a valley outside Mecca where most of th ceremonies connected with the pilgrimage are performed, including throwing stone at the devil and the sacrifices.

مدينا *madína*] cf. B 167, note.

The route above described is the most direct from Sokoto to Mecca. Afte

Iẓan mu tashi da nan mun yi himma   mu ẓo mu kutarkushi amusa da kaia
Iẓan mu ẓo kuturkushi munka tashi   mu ratsa ta zaría amubersu dama
Mu ratsa kano da bauchi mu bersu hauni   mu ẓo mu kurarafa amusa da kaia
Iẓan mun tashi da nan mun yi himma   mu ẓo mu madangana gulbin wukari
Iẓan mun tashi da nan mun yi himma   mu bishi amuyi gabbas hai adamawa
Iẓan mun tashi da nan adamawa   mu ẓo mu kasan bagu amusa da kaia
Shi kaimu garin da babu rashi ga ḳowa   shikin dadi mu sadda da larabawa
Iẓan mun ẓo fa munar munka futa   mu ẓagi makka hai mu wushi madína
Muna ẓuba eṣṣallati bisa muhammad   da aliyan muhammadu ya fi kowa
Ṣahaba nai da tabii tabiína   muna yi muna addua amusami tsira

Kamal ḳaṣidat as-safar ism almukátib ramaḷan bin yusuf bihamd lillaḥi wa husn 'auniḥi as-salat wa as-salam ala rasul allaḥi

---

leaving Adamawa the pilgrims would pass through Baghirmi, Wadai, and Darfur. Crossing the Nile near Khartoum they would go *via* Souakim or Massowah and thence by boat to Jeddah. As most of the pilgrims are also traders, it is more usual to diverge from the direct path in order to visit places such as Kano and Zaria, etc. which the pilgrim is here directed to pass by.

The inscription at the end is in Arabic. السلاة *assalat* should be written الصلاة *aṣṣalat* "prayer" or "salutation."

POEM F.

F In the name of God, the Compassionate, the Merciful; may the peace of God be upon him, after whom there is no prophet.
We thank the glorious King, the mighty One, exalted, glorious and all-powerful.
We further salute Mohammed and his family and friends and all the prophets;
And the followers of his followers, and his friends; and the angels too we greet.
And after we have completed (our) salutations and greetings, do ye listen O companions of Abd-el-Kadr.
And you, my brother, my friend, fear our Lord who made everything.
You my friend, give attention with your ears; the thing which I tell thee is indeed true.
Give up also evil doing and suspicion and envy; give up all proud looks and all abuse.
Repent, leave off all that which is forbidden and speaking evil of God, leave off falsehood, fear to whisper evil about anyone.

THE author of this poem, as also of E, was Sheikh Othman of Sokoto, the conqueror of Hausaland; cf. E, introduction. It was composed in 1802 but first committed to writing by his brother Abd-illahi in 1843. The first sheet, which is in a different handwriting to the rest of the poem, contains several mistakes of transcription.

It consists of introductory prayer, 1—4; exhortation to pay attention and to repent, 5—13; God is the giver of all, 14—16; warnings against hypocrisy, stinginess, covetousness and pride, 17—25; the author's purpose in writing, 26—27; warnings against vain-glory and giving heed to the revilings of men, 28—36; the world is but transitory, 37—39; women should observe modesty, 40—42; all the prophets from Adam to Mohammed have passed away, 43—53; the leaders too amongst the heathen have passed away and have become poor, 54—64; exhortation to follow Mohammed and to make preparation for the journey to the next world, 65—75; none can save thee from dying, 76—79; though they may lament thee when dead, 80—84; the preparations that will be made for thy burial, 85—100; the two angels will come to examine thee in the tomb, 101—110; on the day of resurrection thou shalt arise, when the wicked shall receive punishment, 111—119; appeal for help will be made in vain to Adam, Noah, Abraham, and Jesus, 120—127; Mohammed alone will render aid, 128—136; evil deeds will be compensated for by suffering, 137—142; the narrow bridge which all must cross, 143—145; at its seven turns seven questions will be asked, 146—152; the good will cross safely, the wicked will fall into the fire, 153—163; the different divisions of hell and those who shall inhabit each, with details of tortures to be endured, 164—213;

POEM F.

Bismi alláḥi errahmáni errahími — ṣalla alláḥu ala man la nabíya ba'daḥu
Mu godi jalla saṛki maiíyawa — ta'ala jalla maiíyawa da kowa
Muna kuma yin ṣallati bisa muhammad — da ali da ṣahibi da jama'u annabawa
Da tabii tabiína da waliäu — da malaku muna kuma salmawa
Fa baia shikawa ṣallatu da salmawa — ku sorara jama'a alḳadirawa
Fa ya kai tsan uwana ṣahibina — ka tsorshi ubangíjìmu da ya yi kowa
Abokina ka kakartsa kunuwa naka — abinda na ki fatsa maka babu wawa
Ka ber kuma hasada da matsinna da ḳita — harára duka ka ber ẓagi fa kowa
Ka tuba ka ber harámu du da ṣuabo — ka ber ḳaria ka tsorshi ratsa da kowa

---

the rewards which await the righteous on their entrance into heaven, 214—241; the friends of Mohammed will be there, 242—249; the respect due to his parents prevents the author from going on the pilgrimage, 250—253; conclusion, 254—256.

It will be noticed that every line in this poem ends with the syllable وا *wa*. In chanting this would be specially emphasized and drawn out. The poem contains a larger proportion of Arabic words than any other. Only those Arabic words are as a rule referred to in the notes which have no claim to be regarded as adopted Hausa words. As in E ش *sh* is constantly used for ث *ch*.

2. تعلى *ta'ala*] "exalted," cf. Ar. تعالى *ta'ála* VI. form of علا *'alá* "to be high."

4. ولياع *waliäu*] should be ولياه *waliyáḥu* Ar. "his friends."

5. القادراوا *alḳadirawa*] cf. E 4, note.

6. طن *tsan*] for دن *dan* "son." ط *ts* is frequently substituted for د *d* in this poem, cf. in following line فطا *fatsa* for فدا *fada*. The expression "son of my mother" is simply one of endearment and does not imply actual relationship.

طرش *tsorshi*] "fear," so in line 20. Several different forms of this occur, cf. line 9 ظرش *tsorshi*, line 17 سرث *sorchi*, D 8 ثورو *choro*, line 22 طورن *tsoron*, the last form is the one most commonly used in colloquial Hausa.

7. ككرط *kakartsa*] the more common form is كركت *karkatta* "to bend the head so as to listen intently," cf. B 38, D 32.

8. مطن *matsinna*] Ar. مظنة *matsinnat* "suspicion."

F Leave off too making (wanton) play according to your desire, and your ev intention; leave off gambling, cease taking your fill of everything.
Give up all playing of 'darra' and 'dirka' and stealing, fear the meetin with Him who has power over all.
Repent, give up slandering and jesting; repent, give up going about beggin for everything.
Repent and give up all evil speaking and covetousness; give up all adulter and practising deceit on anyone.
If you would ask for what you want, ask God, for He is rich and the give of everything.
For He will give to thee, He will not be angry; for He is mighty, and H gives strength;
For He listens to him who calls; He is indeed gracious and refuses not.
Repent, cease from unlawful gain, give tithes; fear the meeting with Hin who has power over all.
If thou givest not tithes prepare for the fire; it will destroy you withou doubt.
And the verse (of the Koran beginning with) 'Those who hoard up treasures is the reason, if there is anyone who asks.
Give up taking the property of orphans, fear the meeting with Him wh has power over all.
(The Koran saith) 'Go not near the property of the orphan'; this is th reason if there is anyone who asks.
Repent, leave off seeking after thine own greatness; let thy greatness fea Him who is all powerful.
If thou fearest the King who is almighty, thou wilt be following after thin own greatness, and that without doubt.

---

10. هوا *ḥawa*] Ar. هوى *ḥawá* "eager desire."

شاشا *shasha*] usually written ثاثا *chacha*, a gambling game played with cowrie or ground-nuts.

11. در دك *darra duka*] so original MS., the second د *d* has been omitte in the reproduction. For meaning of *darra* cf. E 16, note.

دركا *dirka*] a game for the purpose of discovering secrets, played by fortune tellers, &c.

12. قزمن *ḳizman*] cf. Ar. قزم *ḳazam* "to accuse."

ددث *dadachi*] "jesting," probably from Ar. دد *dad* with Hausa nominal suffix ث *chi*, cf. *anamimanchi* in following line.

13. انممنثى *anamimanchi*] in D 7 this is spelt اننمنثى *ananminchi*, cf Ar. نمّ *namm* "to slander."

14. غنى *gani*] Ar. "to be rich."

Ka ber kuma yin daria ta ḥawa da suwa   ka ber shasha ka ber ḳoshin ga kowa
Ka bèr darra duka da dirka duka da sata   ka tsorshi gamu da maiiko da kowa
Ka tuba ka ber fa ḳizman ka yi dadachi ba   ka tuba ka ber yawon roḳo ga kowa
Ka tuba da anamimanchi duka da rowa   ka ber zina duka da tsalimshi ga kowa
Kadan roḳo ka ki so roḳo allaḥ   ẓama shi ni gani mabaya kowa
Ẓama shi ni ka baka ba ya fusata   ẓama shi ni azízu da bai gaẓawa
Zama shi ni samiʻu ga mainadäi   fa shi ni ko karímu da ba hannawa
Ka tuba ka ber riba ka bada zaka   ka sarshi gamu da maiiko da kowa
Kadan ba ka fa zaka kowa ka shiria   wuta akaza kassheka fa babu wawa
Fa aiar wallaẓina yaknizuna   dalíli ko akan maitanbaiawa
Ka ber shi dukia yaya marayu   ka tsorshi gamu da maiiko da kowa
Wa la dai taḳrabu mál alyatími   dalíli ko akan maitanbaiawa
Ka tuba ka ber bidan fa girmamaka   fa girman naka tsoron maiíyawa
Kadan ka tsorshi sarki maiíyawa   abika agirmamaka fa babu wawa

---

16. سميع *samiʻu*] Ar. "hearer," an epithet constantly applied to God. مينداع *mainadäi*] "one who calls," cf. Ar. ندو *nada* "to call." The ع is added by mistake, as in line 4.

18. زكا *zaka*] Ar. زكاة *zakat* "alms," in Hausa usually denotes a tithe.

19. ايار *aiar*] should be اية *aiat*, Ar. a verse of the Koran. The verse here quoted is taken from Surah ix. 34 "Those who hoard up gold and silver and do not spend it in the way of God, announce to them the tidings of a grievous punishment."

20. شي *shi*] for ثي *chi*.

21. There are two verses in the Koran beginning with these words, Surah vi. 153 and xvii. 36. دى *dai* does not occur in either, it is probably intended as the Hausa particle "indeed."

23. ابيك *abika*] a passive imperative form "let there be a following after by thee."

F And the verse which begins 'Behold the noblest of you' is indeed a reason if there is anyone who asks.
Leave off that which is evil, work according to the tradition of Mohammed who excels our prophets and excels everyone.
The purpose of the whole of this song is (to commend) the Koran; this is its purpose if there is anyone who asks.
My friend, thou knowest my ignorance; I love the messenger of God who excels all.
Cast out of thy heart the desire to have things given to thee; the glorious One will give to thee, He is the giver of all.
Give up being hastily angry, my brother; thou lovest that it should be said to thee, Thou excellest all.
Thou art proud because it is said thou excellest all; thou revilest men, alas, thou fool.
Men praise thee therefore, in order that thou mayest give them something; they say of thee, This man excels all.
Thou swellest with pride, thou fool; thus the world deceiveth (thee).
When thou hearest its words, my brother, repent; leave off saying thou excellest all.
When anyone in the world revileth or abuseth thee, regard it not, for the sake of the exalted and mighty One.
Why dost thou then speak evil? The exalted and mighty King beholdeth thee.
Wilt thou then give heed to my warning? fear the meeting with Him who has power over all.
Thou lovest the world, my friend, which is passing away; behold the prophets, there is not one (left).
Look back to Adam, to all (the prophets and) Seth; they have gone to the place of Him who has power over all.
Where is Edris, Noah and Hud? they have gone to the place of the mighty King.

---

24. The verse here quoted is taken from Surah xlix. 13 "Behold the noblest of you in the sight of God is the most pious of you."

حقيقا *haḳîḳa*] Ar. "truly" is not a part of the quotation, but is here used as a Hausa word.

25. بدعا *bid'a*] Ar. بدعة *bid'at*, lit. "anything new," so "that which is evil."

26. ورغ *worga*] a Sokoto usage for ونن *wonan;* in Katsena ووغ *woga* is used.

27. بيغى *baigi*] Ar. بيغ *bâg* "to devote oneself entirely to."

28. سن اباك *son abaka*] "the desire that it may be given to thee," or we may perhaps read *suna baka* "they gave thee."

Fa aiyar en akramakum haḳíḳa   dalíli ko akan maitanbaiawa
Ka ber bid'a ka aikata sunna ahmad   fiyayin annabinmu da ya fi kowa
Dalíli worga waḳa duka ga ḳuran   dalíli ko akan maitanbaiawa
Abokina ka sanni jaḥilína   ina baigi rasulu da ya fi kowa
Ka fidda fa ẓushianka da son abaka   ta'ala shi ka baka shi badi kowa
Ka ber saurin fushi ya dan uwana   kana so wai ashe kai ka fi kowa
Kana kuma kunburawa wai ka fi kowa   kana ẓagi mutane kaito wawa
Mutane na yabonka fa don ka basu   suna she wani kai dai ka fi kowa
Kana kuma shishika girma ya ḥauka   kaman nan dúnia ta ki bada wawa
Fa enda ka jita waya dan uwata   ka tuba ka ber shiawa ka fi kowa
Fa kowa sabika ya ẓagika dúnia   ka ḳali don ta'ala maiíyawa
Fa domi kai kana sabon ta'ala   yina ganinka sarki maiíyawa
Ka son dai kankana jin gargadína   ka tsorshi gamu da maiiko ga kowa
Ka son dúnia mayata shi aboki   ka duba annabawa babu kowa
Ka duba tun ga adamu duka shitu   fa sun taffi enda maiiko da kowa
Enna edrisu nuhu kaẓa da ḥudu   fa sun taffi enda sarki maiíyawa

---

34. قالى *ḳali*] "to regard as a small matter," cf. Ar. قل *ḳall* "to be small."

36. كنكنا *kankana*] equivalent to دكنكا *da kanka* "thou thyself."

37. ميوتا *mayata*] "passing away," so in D 85.

39. ادريس *edrisu*] i.e. Enoch.

كذا *kaẓa*] Ar. "thus," Hausa *hakanan.*

هود *ḥudu*] Hud, probably to be identified with Heber. According to the Koran he was sent as a prophet to the tribe of Ad, an idolatrous tribe of Arabs in ancient times.

F And ye, O women, repent, take the (right) way; fear the meeting with Him who has power over all.

O women, cover over your whole body; fear lest the fire should be the covering of any of you.

The verse (of the Koran which says) "Let them not show (their ornaments)" is sufficient for us, and (the verse which says) "Let them draw (their veils)" is a reason to give to anyone.

Where too is Saleh and Lokman? both of them have gone to the place of the mighty King.

Where again is (Abraham) the friend of God? he too is gone to the place of Him who has power over all.

Where are Isaac and Ishmael? both of them have returned to the realm of the Almighty.

Where are Jacob and all his children? they have gone to the place of Him who has power over all.

Where are Moses and Aaron and Lot? they have gone to the place of the mighty King.

Where are Jesus and Alexander, both of them? They have gone to the place of the mighty King.

Where are David and his son Solomon? they left not the dominion of the world to anyone else.

Thou knowest that all have passed away whither (the world) goeth; thou knowest that the mighty One chooseth not for any (to remain).

Consider the excellency of the prophets; Mohammed our prophet excelleth all.

And (thou seest) the dignity of these prophets; may God grant us to accomplish good works.

Thou knowest that the mighty One chooseth not (that) anyone (should continue); He (is) the exalted and glorious One who has power over all.

Where are the Hulhulanu and Nebuchadnezzar? where is Nimrod, a great man amongst the heathen?

---

41. للب *lulubi*] spelt لضبا *luḷubi* A 28, "a veil from the head to the feet."

42. يبدنون...ولويلر *yabdanuna...walyalri*] should be يبدين...وليضربن *yubdína...walyaḍribna*, cf. Koran c. 24. 31 "Let them not show their ornaments, let them draw their veils over their bosoms."

43. Saleh according to the Koran was sent as a prophet to the idolatrous tribe of Thamud in Arabia, but was rejected by them.

Lokman, a wise man supposed to have been a descendant of Job. He is regarded by some as identical with the Greek Esop.

Fa matan ku tuba ku kama sunna   ku tsorshi gamu da maiiko (da) kowa
Fa matan ku lulubi du jikinku   ku tsorshi fa lulubi na wuta ga kowa
Fa aiar wa yabdanuna fa ta ishimu   da walyalri fa dalíli shi ga kowa
Enna kuma ṣalihu loḳmanu su duka   fa sun taffi enda sarki maiíyawa
Enna kuma shi khalilu allaḥi shi kua   fa ya taffi enda maiiko da kowa
Enna isaḳu ismalilu su duka   fa sun koma ga ẓati maiíyawa
Enna yaḳubu har yayansa su duka   fa sun taffi enda maiiko da kowa
Enna musai da ḥaruna da loṭu   fa sun taffi enda sarki maiíyawa
Enna isa da ẓalḳarnini su duka   fa sun taffi enda sarki maiíyawa
Enna dauda har dansa sulaiman   sarota dúnia ba su ber ga kowa
Ka san duka su taffi duka enda ẓatsa   ka san jabbaru shi bai ẓabi kowa
Ka duba har fiyayan annabawa   muhammadu annabinmu da ya fi kowa
Da alhurman wodanan annabawa   fa allaḥ bamu kikawan shikawa
Ku san jabbaru shi bai ẓabi kowa   ta'ala jalla maiiko da kowa
Enna kuma ḥulḥulanusu bakhtnaṣr   enna nimrudu maiyan káfirawa

---

48. ذالقرنين *ẓalḳarnini*] Alexander the Great.

50. ذاطا *ẓatsa*] the meaning is somewhat obscure. We should probably read ذاتا *ẓata* "will go," and understand دونيا *dúnia* before it.

52. حرمن *hurman*] cf. Ar. حرم *hirm* "dignity."

ككاون *kikawan*] should apparently be عيكاون *aikawan* (cf. MS.) "works."

54. هلهلانس *ḥulḥulanusu*] unintelligible; MS. apparently corrupt.

F Where is the Sheddád, who built the mighty palace? where is Goliath, a grea man amongst the heathen?
Where is Manzur and Iwaja in the world? they like Pharaoh (were) wicke heathen.
Where are Haman and Karun in the world? they had riches, there to-da they have nothing.
Where is Bilkis, the woman who possessed a kingdom? she was a Mussulma she came to see the prophets.
Where are they themselves to-day in the world? they had riches, ther to-day they have nothing.
Where too are Abu Jahl and Harith? where is Walid, a great man amongs the heathen?
Abu Lahab, Moseilima and Obba they are there in hell, to-day they possess nothin
Thou knowest that in the world we stay but a short time, in the othe world we shall continue.
Though thou desirest to be king in this world, thou knowest that tho shalt lie down alone in the tomb.
Consider the great kings, there to-day in the next world they have nothing.
Leave off rejoicing and seeking after this world, thou knowest indeed ho easily it draws thee (away).
Thou knowest how to obtain (good) by following the way of Mohamme and by faith and by the completion of good works.
Repent, seek provisions for the way that thou mayest prepare to make journey, for there is no continuance for anyone.
Because this journey, without preparation made in this world, is troublesom and toilsome to anyone.

---

55. Sheddád son of Ad is said to have built a garden in Arabia in imit tion of Paradise. When it was finished he and his companions set out to se it, but were destroyed by a terrible noise from heaven.

ميقصر *maiḳaṣr*] cf. Ar. قصر *ḳaṣr* "palace" or "castle." Cf. Lat. *castrum.*

مشيد *mashíd*] Ar. lit. "cemented with gypsum," so "strong."

56. فرعون *firauna*] Ar. فرعون *fir'aun* "Pharaoh" or "a tyrant such as Pharao was."

57. هامان *ḥamana*] "Haman." According to the Koran, c. 27. 5, this wa the name of Pharaoh's chief minister.

قارون *ḳaruna*] Karun is to be identified with Korah. According to Mohan medan tradition his opposition to Moses was the result of insolence caused b his immense wealth.

58. بلقيس *bilḳisu*] Bilkis is supposed to have been the name of the queen c Sheba.

ذى *ẓayi*] should be ذو *ẓo* "came."

Enna sheddádu maiḳaṣru almashídi   enna jaluta maiyan káfirawa
Enna manẓur enna iwaju ga dúnia   su firauna miagun káfirawa
Su ḥamana su ḳaruna ga dúnia   da sunka wodata yo shan ba su kowa
Enna bilḳisu mashi da ta yi mulki   da ta msulumta ta ẓayi annabawa
Enna daḳaianusu yo nan ga dúnia   da sunka wodata yo shan ba su kowa
Enna kuma shi abujaḥil da hárich   enna su walidu maiyan káfirawa
Abulaḥbi musailima har ubanu   suna shan a lakhira yo ba su kowa
Ka san dúnia kadan muka jinjimawa   a daki a lakhira muka tabettawa
Kadan ka so ka malika dúniarga   ka san kai dai ka kwantawar kushiwa
Ka dubi sarakuna duka maiamaia   suna shan a lakhira yo ba su kowa
Ka ber murna da neman nan ta dúnia   ka san dai ba wuya ta ka sunbuliwa
Ka san samu ga bin sunnar muhammad   da aiman da kikawar shikawa
Ka tuba ka nemi gúzuri don ka shiria   yinin taffiar da babu ẓama ga kowa
Ẓama taffiar da ba gúẓuri ga dúnia   aẓába shi fa tába shi ga kowa

---

60. Abujahl, one of Mohammed's chief opponents; he was killed at the battle of Bedr.

حارث *hárich*] i.e. Harith VII., prince of the Beni Ghassán.

Al Walid, an enemy of Mohammed. He is said to have been killed by the angel Gabriel for his opposition to Mohammed.

61. Abu Lahab, uncle of Mohammed and his bitter opponent.

Moseilama, a diminutive form of Moslama, who was a rival prophet of Mohammed and was killed at the battle of Yemama.

Obba-ibn-Khalf received a wound from Mohammed at the battle of Ohod from which he afterwards died.

63. دونيرغا *dúniarga*] so line 71. Sokoto use for دونيانن *dúnia nan*.

65. سنبليوا *sunbuliwa*] "draw out," or it should perhaps be *son buliwa* "loves to make trial of," cf. Ar. بلو *bala* "to test."

66. ككاور *kikawar*] should apparently be عيكاوا *aikawa* (cf. MS.) "works."

67. ينن *yinin*] for نين *na yin*.

68. تعبا *tába*] Ar. تعب *ta'ab* "fatigue."

F Thou shalt by no means ever return from this journey; when thou hast set thy face (towards the next world) there is no turning round.
Make preparation, thou art going towards the grave, my brother; when thou comest to it there is no returning again.
Thou knowest that in this world there is no place in which to sit down or to stay; thou wilt leave this place then without doubt.
The world is a city which is and (after a while) is not, thou knowest this world will soon destroy the fool.
If then this world had continued as a city from olden time, thou wouldst meet the messengers (of God) and the prophets.
Look back to Adam; (our) ancestors have all passed away, and Mohammed who excels all.
Hasten to arise from sleep, my brother; fear then the sleep within the tomb.
Fear the day of death which is coming; though thou hast made no preparation, thou wilt certainly (have to) go.
Thy parents and thy brothers will surround thee, they will all come to thee, none of them have any power (to help).
Medicine is brought and put in water and given to thee, they give it thee to drink in order that thou mayest become better.
Thou stretchest thy limbs, thou criest out and groanest; of all who love thee where is one that can help?
Thine eye closes, thy life departs; those who love thee can but pray again.
Some will utter a prayer, some will lament, thou thyself hast set thy face to a place whence is no looking back.
And the dead man's children and wives will lament, the men will say, (Behold) the power of the Almighty.
The men will say, Be patient, cease (lamenting), behold the power of the glorious One, there is no continuance for anyone.
They give not way to tears, for they are powerless, and the mighty King hath power over them.
Where is this greatness of thine and thy lovers? to-day thou liest in the tomb.

---

70. برزخ *barzakhu*] Ar. "time between death and resurrection," "tomb."
ويووا *woiwuwa*] for ويوياوا *woiwoiawa*, as in line above.

72. بد *bada*] according to Abd-el-Kadr we should read *bata* "destroy." Cf. B 108, note; or *bada wawa* may be equivalent to "deceives," cf. line 32.

73. The sense is somewhat uncertain; the argument apparently being "If this world were like a city whose inhabitants changed not, you would meet now all who have ever lived in it."

78. احقا *ajiḳa*] lit. "it is moistened."
فدم *fa dom*] must be intended for فدن *fa don.*
عفوا *afua*] cf. III. form of Ar. عفو *'afá* "to restore to health."

Bali taffiar tutut ba ẓaka koma   kadan ka sa gabba ba woiwoiawa
Ka shiria ẓaka barzakhu dan uwana   kadan ka je ka ba koma da woiwuwa
Ka san dúniarga babu bigri ka ẓamna   gari nan ẓaka bershi fa babu wawa
Tana da kamar gari kowa ba gari ba   ka san dúniarga maẓa ta ka bada wawa
Fa en dai dâ gari shi dúniarga   ka iski mursalína da annabawa
Ka duba tun ga adamu awalinsu   fa sun taffi har ga ahmada ya fi kowa
Ka razana dagga kwana dan uwata   ka tsorshi fa kunshia ta shikin kushiwa
Ka tsorshi fa randa mutua ta ishima   da ba ka shiri fa ka taffi babu wawa
Iyayi yan uwaka su ki wuyka   su taro agareka du kan ba maiíyawa
Akawa magani ajiḳa abaka   su baka ka sha fa dom fa ka sami afua
Kana mika kana ḳara da nishi   masowa duk enna maitaimakawa
Ido shim birkishi raia fishima   masowa naka sai kuma salmawa
Wodansu suna ṣallati wonsu kuka   fa kai ka sa gabba ba woiwoiwa
Da yarayi da matayi ka kuka   maẓa na she fa iko maiíyawa
Maẓa na she ku ḥanḳuri akan ku daina   fa iko jalla babu ẓama ga kowa
Suna ḳarfi halli don ba su iko   fa yan ikonsa sarki maiíyawa
Enna girmanga naka enna masowa   fa yo kai dai ka kuntawa kushiwa

---

79. مسوا *masowa*] usually pronounced *masoiya*, pl. of *maso* "a lover."

80. شم *shim*] a Sokoto use for شن *shina*, cf. line 78.

81. ونس *wonsu*] a shortened form of ودنس *wodansu* "some."

82. يارايى *yarayi*] an irregular plural of *yaro* "child," the usual form being يارا *yara*; so too *matayi* for *mata*.

84. قرفى حلى *ḳarfi halli*] lit. "they have a strong disposition," i.e. "they do not give way to crying."

فين ايكو نس *fa yan ikonsa*] lit. "they are children of His power, the mighty King."

F Where is the protection on the part of those who praised thee? to-day they carry thee to the place of burial.
Truly it was falsehood they spake concerning thee, they loved thee not; (even though) they love thee, thou hast no power to-day.
A small piece of white cloth is brought and prepared, it is completely sewn and joined together.
Some will arise and go thus to the grave, wood is cut for the grave.
Water is brought for thee, the washing is completed, thou art washed and cleaned for burial.
A shroud is made for thee, thou art wrapped therein, thou art taken out of thy house, thou fool.
A line (of men) is formed, the saying of prayer is completed, alas, thou knowest not what is done, thou fool.
When they have finished praying they take thee, and carry thee, and thrust thee into the grave.
A little piece of wood is brought and is secreted; some place pots also, or treasures.
A little new grass is brought and pressed down; by the feet of all is thy grave pressed down.
Earth is mixed and kneaded up again; dry earth is brought (and placed) above the tomb.
They wash their hands thus and their feet, they all salute one another.
They scatter in silence, they leave thee in the grave; thou thyself criest but there is no coming out.
Thy goods are divided, rejoicing is made, thy goods are given to thy children, each is given something.
Thou art forgotten, no share is put out for thee; the pain in the tomb is sufficient for thee.
The angels Nakir and Munkari come forth to thee, thou art in thy grave alone, no one is with thee.

---

86. قرير *karaiar*] "protection of," the final ر *r* being used instead of ن *n*; or we may read *karia* "where are the lies spoken by..."

سو نى اكيك *su ni akaika*] apparently equivalent to *su ni kaika* "they carry thee."

88. دن فرى *dan fari*] lit. "son of white," i.e. small piece of white (cloth). For similar use of *dan* cf. lines 94, 95.

89. It is customary to place small branches of trees in the grave with the corpse, coffins not being used.

90. ما *ma*] for *maka*.

الضوا *allowa*] washing before praying, cf. Ar. وضو "an ablution."

91. لكفنى *likafani*] "winding sheet," cf. Ar. كفن *kafan*. The *l* must be

Enna ḳaraiar fa masuyabonka kulum   fa yo su ni akaika wurin kushiwa
Ashe ḳaria su ki maka ba su sonka   fa sun so ba ka iko yo da kowa
Akawo dan fari kuma ẓa ashiria   adumka duk ana kuma gangamawa
Wodansu su tashi ẓasu haḳan kushiwa   anasaran itashi don kushiwa
Akama ma rua agama da alḷowa   awanki ka fa gaslu ẓaman kushiwa
Asa maka dan likafani kuma asunḳi   afishika ga dakin naka wawa
Atsaida saffu aṣṣalla shika kaito   fa kai ba ka san abinda akai ba wawa
Idan sun ḳari ṣalla kuma su doka   su kaika su ẓonkutsaka shikin kushiwa
Akawo dan itashi kuma ajira   tukani wonsu ko suka alaẓawa
Akawo dan haki ganyi aduntsi   kafafi duk aduntsima kushiwa
Akwaba ḳasa ana kuma lalabawa   ajawo ḳiḳasasa akan kushiwa
Su wanki hanuansu kaẓa ḳafafu   suna kuma gaisuar jiuna ga kowa
Su washi shíu su berka chikin kushiwa   ka kuka dakanka babu wurin fitowa
Araraba dukiarka adora murna   fa yayaya abasu abaiwa kowa
Fa anmanta dakai ba afidda naka   aẓába ta ishika shikin kushiwa
Nakiri da munkari su fito gareka   kana ḳabrinka kai dai babu kowa

---

the Arabic article *al*, which has become part of the word in Hausa, cf. *lafia* from Ar. *'afiat*.

92. lit. "a line is made to stand up."

94. دن اتاشي *dan itashi*] lit. "a son of wood," i.e. a little piece of wood; cf. *dan haki* in following line.

تكاني *tukani*] pl. of *tukunia* "a cooking pot." Broken pots are often placed in the grave with the corpse.

95. غنيي *ganyi*] for غيني *gainyi* "fresh."

98. شو *shíu*] equivalent to شرو *shiru* "silently," cf. B 54.

101. For account of examination of the dead in the grave cf. D 41, note.

F If thou art a believer thou wilt answer, and the joy of the Lord will fill the whole tomb.
The frankincense of heaven and its pleasures (will be thine), and the Houris will walk within thy tomb.
And the angels will rejoice with thee there, in the light where is no darkness or loneliness.
If thou art a profligate thou wilt see humiliation; Nakir (and his companion) will turn thee over in the grave.
They will beat thee till thou art sore; thou wilt cry, but help will be refused.
They will beat thee with sticks and whips; thou wilt groan, where will there be any to help?
The tomb will press thee, they will beat thee, thou wilt remain there constantly without turning.
Scorpions and snakes will gather together, and with insects will pour forth poison.
They will bite thee then, thou wilt have no power to turn, thou wilt remain there continually alone.
Thou wilt remain therefore till the resurrection day; on that day the glorious One will raise up every one.
The trumpet shall sound, all shall rise and at once come to the place of standing.
And a line of fifty thousand shall be made, by the glorious and mighty King.
The sun will draw nigh and send forth heat upon men; it will burn their heads, it will split them.
And those who have committed sin will on that day be ashamed; they will have an evil odour poured upon them.
And hypocrites and evil-doers shall be ashamed; with them shall be gathered all the heathen.
There shall be crying and thirst and hunger, alas; they are pierced through (with pain), none of them have any to help.
The angels of the fire will surround them all, by the power of the glorious and mighty King.
There will be weeping each for himself, and there will be no helper at all for you.

---

103. حور العينِ *huru-l-'ini*] Ar. lit. "antelopes with large eyes." In Arabic poetry women are frequently called antelopes or gazelles. According to Mohammedan tradition each believer will have seventy-two of these Houris as wives, cf. line 228.

105. ذلا *ẓilla*] Ar. ذلّ *ẓull* "humiliation."

106. كوشيكشيا *kushikushia*] usually applied to itch on the hands or feet.

Izan dai mumini ka ka kai jawaba   fa nima er-rabbu ta shika du kushiwa
Turari duk na aljenna da nima   da huru-l-'ini na yawo kushiwa
Malaiku suna murna da kai shan   shikin an-núr fa babu dufu da kiwa
Idan kua fasiḳi ka ka ka ga ẓilla   nakiri suki wuiyaka shikin kushiwa
Suna dirkanka har kushikushia   kana kuka anamanáa gaẓawa
Kulakin ḳarfuna suka ẓunbudama   kana nishi ana maitaimakawa
Kushiwa ta matsika suna bugunka   ka ẓamna nan tutur ba jirkitáwa
Kunamai duk su gaia mashiẓai   da sususi deffi su ka bungulawa
Su chia fa ba ka iko jirkitáwa   ka zamna nan tutur kuma babu kowa
Ka ẓamna nan fa har ranan ḳiama   yini nan jalla kua shi ka tada kowa
Abusa ḳafo antashi duk atashi   fa saa dai ataru wurin tsaia
Saffu kua har dubu khamsin akanyi   da iko jalla sarki maiíyawa
Fa rana ta kusa töi akan mutani   tana ḳona fa kainua na fashiwa
Fa masuzina fa ranan su ka kumia   suna doii mugunya na ẓuba
Munafiḳai da fasiḳai ka kumia   su tarua da su da jama'u al-káfirawa
Anakuka ḳishirua kaito junwa   anasoki babu duk manáa gaẓawa
Malaiku wuta sun kiwoiyi duk   da ikon jalla sarki maiíyawa
Anakuka fa kowa ana ta kai nasa   fa ba maitaimaka maku babu kowa

---

109. بنغلاوا *bungulawa*] a Sokoto word, "pour forth," cf. line 190.

111. ينى *yini*] lit. "the time remaining till evening," or "to continue doing anything till evening." Here used in ordinary sense of "a day."

117. جنوا *junwa*] for ينوا *yunwa*, pronounced *yungwa*, "hunger."

اناسك *anasoki*] lit. "it is pierced through." The sense of the remaining words is obscure, lit. "not all hinder help."

F If there be a long delay on the day of the resurrection, they will go to the messengers (of God) and the prophets,
In order that they may go to the glorious King, the most glorious One who has power over everything.
They will say, O Adam, thou art our father, do thou seek salvation for us from the Almighty.
He will say on that day, I myself have no power, only Noah has such.
(If you) go to Noah, he will say, O men, go to the Friend (of God), the faithful one who has (all) power.
(If you) go to Abraham, the Friend (of God), he too will say, I have no power to-day to save anyone;
Go to Moses, my brethren; he will go to the glorious One who has power over all.
If you go to him, he will say, Go back to Jesus, he will go to the almighty King.
If you go to Jesus, he will say, Go back to Mohammed, our prophet, who excels all.
For he is the protector of sinners, Mohammed, the believer in God, who excels all.
They will go to him and say to him, O Mohammed, who excellest all, seek for us salvation.
He will say, (Behold my) relations, O glorious King, O Thou who promisest that which is true, Thou art almighty.
He will speak, he will prostrate himself in the presence of the King; he will say, These are my people, O almighty One.
It will be said to him, Raise thyself up, O Mohammed, there is no prostration to-day for thee, who excellest all.
And that which thou desirest we give thee, O Mohammed, we choose thee, who excellest all.
He will say, I desire salvation, O God, most glorious and almighty.
God will say, Let it be granted to thee; verily we desire judgment for all, by the power of the glorious King the almighty One.

---

120. سيى *saiyi*] lit. "a temporary booth or covering for the night," used here for "a delay."

121. ايسذو *aisuẓo*] apparently intended for اذوس *aẓosu* "let them go" or "they will go."

124. امين *amini*] Ar. "faithful."

125. شسى *shi si*] apparently intended for شثى *shi ché* "he says."

سر *sar*] for طر or طير *tsira* "saves."

129. شفيع *shafi'u*] Ar. "mediator" or "protector."

مذنبين *muẓnibina*] Ar. "sinners," cf. *ẓanba* "crime," E 25.

Ida(n) fa saiyi ḳiama tsawita   azo da ga mursalina da amabawa
Fa domin aisuẓo sun ga jalla sarki   fa jalla jallan maiiko da kowa
Su she ya adamu kai ni ubamu   ka nimo á gajinmu ga maiíyawa
Shi she yo ba ni iko ko ga kaina   fa saiko nuhu ko fa shina íyawa
Aẓo fa ga nuhu shi che mutane   ku ẓo ga khalilu amini maiíyawa
Aẓo ga khalilu ibraḥima shi kua   shi si yo ba ni iko sar da kowa
Ku ẓo ku ga musai ya ku yan uwana   shi ẓo shi ga jalla maiiko da kowa
Idan anẓo gareshi ya she ku koma   ga isai shi je ga sarki maiíyawa
Idan anẓo ga isai ya she ku koma   ga ahmadu annabinmu da ya fi kowa
Ẓama shini shafi'u al-muẓnibina   aminu allaḥi ahmada ya fi kowa
Aẓo gareshi ashe masa ya muhammad   bido shetonmu kai ni ka fi kowa
Shina she umati ya jalla sarki   mawa'adu ka haḳḳ kai ni maiíyawa
Shi fadi shina sujuda inda ẓati   shina she umati ya maiíyawa
Ashe masa tasa kanka fa ya muhammad   fa babu sujuda yo kai ka fi kowa
Fa mi ka ka so mu baka fa ya muhammad   fa mun ẓabika kai ni ka fi kowa
Shi je jeto na ki so ya-llaḥuma   fa jalla jallana maiiko da kowa
Ashe anbaka ai mu so du hisabli   da ikon jalla sarki maiíyawa

---

131. موعد *mawa'adu*] "one who promises," cf. Ar. وعد *wa'ad* "to promise."

132. سجود *sujuda*] Ar. "to make a prostration," usually spelt *sajada*, cf. D 34. In Arabic *sujud* would be the verbal noun, and *sajada* the perfect.

ذاتى *ẓati*] in F 45 *ẓati* is equivalent to "realm," here apparently it means "king."

135. شجى جيتو *shi je cheto*] for شثى ثيتو *shi che cheto*.

ياللهم *ya-llaḥuma*] "O God." The MS. is here very indistinct, but this seems the most probable reading.

136. حسابلى *hisabli*] should perhaps be حساب نى *hisabi ni*, cf. MS. "judgment." Cf. Ar. حساب *hisáb*.

F And the will of God shall bring together all creatures, it will bring them to the fire without doubt.

For (the saying) "And thy Lord shall come" is true, and this verse (of the Koran) is a (sufficient) reason to (give to) anyone.

The judgment is completed, actions are weighed; the balance is brought for everything.

We shall be placed according to the list of our deeds; the Mussulmans will cleave to the right hand.

Hypocrites and profligates shall cry out; (in accordance with) their list (of deeds) they shall cleave to the left hand.

They shall begin to call out, (they shall have) trouble (upon) trouble, pain shall come upon them, without doubt.

The bridge shall be set up in the fire, men shall ascend upon it by the power of the Almighty.

And its sharp edge and slipperiness shall pierce them; its path is (as fine as) a hair, without doubt.

It takes many thousands of years (to cross); its height and its length is the same, without doubt.

The bridge, we understand, has seven turns, and the questions asked at each are all different.

Behold, at the first turn thou wilt hear (the question concerning) the unity (of God); thou wilt be still further questioned, without doubt.

At the second thou wilt hear (the question) about purification, at the third about prayer, at the fourth about fasting, without doubt.

At the fifth turn thou wilt hear of giving tithes; thou wilt be further questioned, without doubt.

At the sixth turn thou wilt hear of obedience to parents, thou fool; thou wilt be further questioned, without doubt.

(Thou wilt be asked if thou hast) bidden (men to do that which is) good and kept them back from evil; this is the seventh question for each.

When thou hast reached all (the turns) on the resurrection day, thou shalt remain there in the heavenly home.

---

137. قدرا *ḳudira*] Ar. قدر *ḳadar* "destiny," "will of God."

138. The quotation is from Surah lxxxix. 23, "Thy Lord shall come and the angels, rank by rank."

140. ايك *aiku*] "deeds," plural of *aiki*. In previous line ايكا *aiuka* occurs as its plural.

141. Or we should perhaps translate "they will hold their list in the left hand," and in the previous line "the Mussulmans will hold theirs in the right hand."

143. Lit. "there shall be going up, there shall be ascending by the power..."

Fa ḳudira ta gabato talikai duk
jaḥannama ta gabato babu wawa

Ẓama fa waja‘a rabbuka shi haḳiḳa
fa aia nan dalili shi ga kowa

Aḳari ko hisabi har aiuka
awunsu nan akai da mizani ga kowa

Ajefo har takardun aiku namu
musulmi nasu dama su ki riḳawa

Munafiḳai da fasiḳai ka kuka
takardu nasa hauni su ki rikawa

Su dora kira chabura ya chabura
aẓaba ta ishesu fa babu wawa

Fa ankafa kua ṣirati chikin jahíma
atashi ahau da ikon maiiyawa

Da kaifi kua da samtsi duk za soka
ḳaramta taswa gashi babu wawa

Dubu kua har alif shekara kutumshi
hawa nasa har sawo nasa babu wawa

Ṣirati mun ji toẓo ni bokkoi ni
fa su duka tanbaia banbam ga kowa

Ga toẓo ni nafari ko akaji tauhída
akan kuma tanbaiarka fa babu wawa

Nabiu luḻḻo fa ṣalla ka ji näuku
nafutsu fa ka ji aẓumi babu wawa

Ga toẓo fa nabiar ka ji zaka
akan kuma tanbaiarka fa babu wawa

Na shidda fa bin iyayi ka ji wawa
akan kuma tanbaiarka fa babu wawa

Da amru da kiota kuma da ḥanna da munkar
akan kuma tambaia na bokkoi ga kowa

Kadan ka ẓo da su duk ran ḳiama
giddan aljenna shan ka ka tabettawa

---

144. تسو *taswa*] a lengthened form of تى *tai* or تس *tas* "its."

145. Lit. "a thousand even to a thousand years is its likeness."

147. توحيد *tauhída*] cf. A 48, note.

148. لضوا *luḻḻo*] apparently another form of *alwaḻḻa* "purification," the *l* or *al* being the Arabic article, and the original root being Ar. وضو.

151. Lit. "and of the commanding of good and again of the preventing of evil."

امر...منكر *amru...munkar*] Ar. "command...a thing which is disgraceful."

F If thou reachest not and completest not indeed all of them thus; thou knowest that thou wilt roll into the fire.

Some will pass the bridge like a wind, some like lightning, without doubt.

Some will go over running, some going slowly, some crawling.

They shall enter hell (Jahannam) and shall be burned; as for all of them there shall be chains of fire for each.

All the believers shall pass over; all the profligates shall fail to pass over.

The verse (of the Koran) "They shall be driven who...," in the chapter Zumara, is a reason (to give) to anyone.

It shall be said to them, No messengers (of God) shall come to you; they shall say, Alas! they shall understand that there is no contending for anyone.

It will be said to them, Fall into the fire and remain there constantly, there is no death any more at all for anyone.

(The verse which says) "Enter" is sufficient for thee, if there be anyone who asks a reason.

They will bite their fingers (in their) remorse, they will say, Alas for us to-day they have nothing.

And the verse which says "And on the day when the evil-doer shall bite," is sufficient for thee, if there be anyone who asks a reason.

They shall be brought to Laza, to Sakar and Hutama, they shall enter Säir without doubt.

They shall be brought to Jahím, Hawiya and Falaka, they shall meet with pain, they shall roll (in the fire).

And when they reach Hawiya, a division shall take place there; they shall be brought to different places in which to remain.

Those who are proud shall be brought to their place; in Bulisa, I understand, shall they remain.

And the whisperers of evil shall be brought to an evil-smelling place; in Jifi, I understand, shall they remain.

---

154. شوطرو *shutsirwa*] "to pass away," a more common form is شودى *shudi.*

158. The quotation is from Surah xxxix. 71 and 73, "They who have disbelieved will be driven into hell in bands,...and those who have feared their Lord shall be driven into paradise in bands."

زمر *zumra*] should be زمرا *zumará.* "Bands" is used as the title of the Surah.

159. اشى...سجى *ashe...su je*] for اثى...سثى *ache...suche.*

مايكا *maaika*] the prefix *ma* or *mai* is uniformly used in Hausa to denote the noun agent, but in this one case the meaning is passive, i.e. "one sent," not "sender."

161. The quotation is from Surah xxxix. 72, "It shall be said, Enter the gates of hell, abiding therein for ever."

Kadan ba ka ẓo da tsan fa ḳari su haḳa   ka san kai dai wuta ka ka gangarawa
Ṣirati wonsu kan shutsirwa iska   wodansu ya wolḳia kuma babu wawa
Wodansu kamar gudu wosu sanu sanu   wodansu da jan jiki su ka ḳetariwa
Jaḥannama ẓasu tusga kuma akona   fa su duka sasari na wuta ga kowa
Jama'ar muminai su ka ḳetariwa   jama'ar fasiḳai ba ḳetariwa
Fa aiar shanta wasiḳa ellaẓina   ga suratu zumra dalili shi ga kowa
Ashe fa da su maaika ba su isuku   su je wai sun ji babu musuwa ga kowa
Ashe fa da su ku fada wuta ku duma   tutur kuma babu mutua du ga kowa
Fa aiar shana adkhulu ta ishika   dalili ko akan maitanbaiawa
Suna kuma jiẓa yasosi na dama   suna she laitaná yo ba su kowa
Wa yoma ya'aḷḷu at-tsálimu ta ishika   dalili ko akan maitanbaiawa
Akaisu ga latsa har saḳara da hutama   su tusga har sa'ira babu wawa
Akaisu jahíma ḥawia har ga falaḳu   su iski aẓaba shan su ka gangarawa
Fa tunda ga ḥawiya shan akarabasu   akaisu gari gari kuma tabettawa
Akai kuma masugirman kai garinsu   ga bulisa na ji shan su ka tabettawa
Fa masurada akaisu gari na mushi   ga jifia na ji shan su ka tabettawa

---

162. جيذ *jiẓa*] for ثيذ *chiẓa* or *chiẓo* "bite."
ليتنا *laitaná*] Ar. "would that we had...!"

163. The quotation is from Surah xxv. 29, "And on the day when the evil-doer shall bite his hands saying, O, would that I had chosen to follow with the apostle."

164. According to Mohammedan tradition the seven divisions in hell will be assigned as follows: the first, Jaḥannam, to wicked Mohammedans; the second, Laẓa, to the Jews; the third, al-Hutama, to the Christians; the fourth, as-Sa'ír, to the Sabians; the fifth, Saḳar, to the Magians; the sixth, al-Jahím, to idolaters; the seventh, the worst of all, al-Ḥawiya, to hypocrites. Falaka, line 165, is apparently another name for Hawiya; it is perhaps connected with Ar. فلق *falaḳ* "a mountain-cleft."

166. Lit. "they shall be brought, a place, a place, remaining."

F And those who stole the tithes shall be brought to their place in Tukuwia there, I understand, shall they remain.
A hot iron shall be ever (prepared) for them, and (they shall have) pain; it shall be said to them that they all have no helper.
And the verse which says "Those who hoard up treasures," is sufficient and a true reason.
And it says again, "Let them not thus think," this verse is a reason (to give) to anyone.
And all liars shall be taken to their place, in Mansia, I understand, shall they continue.
Those who refused to wash shall be carried to their place in Zamhari, where cold shall destroy them.
It will break their bones, it will cut all their limbs, it will cut all the veins of the heathen.
They shall cry aloud, an angel shall afflict them, and (they shall have) fire and great cold, without doubt.
(Such an one) will say, O angel, they will pray for death, (that) they (may) obtain deliverance from the fire and may obtain respite.
The verse which says "And they cried out," is sufficient for you, if there be anyone who asks a reason.
And the verse which says "continue" and "abide" is a reason, in the fire shall they remain.
And the profligates shall be taken to (their) evil place, in the back part of the fire shall they continue.
They shall be brought to Yalamlama, they shall see pain, and to Habhaba, where they shall continue.
They shall be brought to Waila, it is a bank of fire, in Wadilgayi shall they continue.
They shall go to Lakabira, there shall they fall, scorpions shall meet them there.
And there will be dogs to bark in the fire, they will bark and tear and cry.

---

171. For quotation here referred to cf. line 19, note.

172. The quotation is from Surah iii. 172, "Let not those who have disbelieved think that the delay which we have granted them is a gain to themselves."

174. ميفساوا *maifasawa*] lit. "splitting open."

176. زمهري *zamḥari*] according to the commentators on Surah xxxix. 72 the only alleviation which will be granted to those in hell will be that they will be taken out of the fire to drink boiling water and to suffer *zamḥari*, i.e. extreme cold.

178. The quotation is from Surah xxxviii. 2, "How many generations have we destroyed before them, then they cried out and it was no time of escape."

Akai kuma masuchin zaka garinsu   ga tukuwia na ji shan kuma tabettawa
Ana masu lalas har abbada aẓaba   ashe masu ba su duk maitaimakawa
Fa aiar wallaẓina yaknizuna   fa ta issa kua dalili babu wawa
Wa aiḻa kuma kaẓa la yahsibanna   fa aiar nan dalili shi ga kowa
Akai kuma masuḳaria da garinsu   fa mansia na ji su ka tabettawa
Akai kuma masuḳi luḷḷo garinsu   ga zamḫari enda sanyi maifasawa
Shi karya ḳasshi shi yenki duk gabobi   shi yenki duk jiwoji káfirawa
Su dora kira fa malika ya batansu   fa ḳuma wuta da zamḫari babu wawa
Shi je ya malika su roḳi mutua   su sami fita wutar ga su samu afua
Fa aiar shan fa nada ta ishiku   dalili ko akan maitanbaiawa
Fa aiar mákithína da lábithína   dalili nan wuta su ka tabettawa
Fa masuzina akaisu garin mugunya   ga ta dabarun wuta su ka tabettawa
Akaisu yalamlamu su gano aẓaba   fa har ḫabḫabu shan su ka tabettawa
Akaisu ga wailu wuta zazan wuta je   ga wadilgayi shan su ka tabettawa
Su tusga lakabira shan su fada   kunamai mai ashan fa su ki ishiwa
Da karnuka chikin wuta masuhafshi   suna hafshi suna yaga da tsawa

---

179. The quotation in which *mákithína* occurs is from Surah xviii. 2, "They shall have a fair reward, wherein they shall continue for ever."

The second quotation, in which *lábithína* occurs, is from Surah lxxviii. 23, "Hell shall be......the home of transgressors to abide therein for ever."

180. غتدبرن *ga ta dabarun*] cf. MS., which is very indistinct; *dabarun* is probably the Ar. دبر *dabr* "back of."

182. زازان *zazan*] explained by Abd-el-Kadr as equivalent to *rafi* "a bank" or "edge."

183. In the latter half of the line the second *mai* should be omitted.

184. ياغا *yagu*] "tear," usually applied to the tearing of paper or cloth.

F The fire too, behold it rages and burns, it breaks the limbs of the heathen.
Fetters and leg-irons of fire shall be placed on them; the fire shall surround them, and (burn them with a) roar.
They (the angels) shall beat all the heathen, they will cry out, help shall be refused.
The angels will lift up bellows, they will increase the fire, (the men) will cry out.
They will be brought up upon a rock to drink hot water; their bowels will be poured out.
Serpents also shall be gathered together to them, and will fight with them and pour out their poison.
They shall be burnt and shall be brought to Sa'uda; it is the rock of torment for the heathen.
And the heathen shall be dragged prostrate to the edge; it will destroy the heathen.
It (stretches) for a thousand years, there are no limits to it; (such is) the height of the rock Sa'uda, in very truth.
They will return in confusion and will mount up; and from thence again will the heathen cry out.
Alas, thence they shall roll down beneath it; in the hot fire shall they roll.
They shall be brought to Laria and to trees of fire, and putrid matter shall be the food of the heathen.
And the verse which says "He shall be given to drink putrid water," is a reason to give if there be anyone who asks.
The fire shall consume them till it eats up their liver; their lungs also and bowels shall be poured out.
Fire too shall come out of their eyes and mouth and nostrils; out of all of them shall fire come abundantly.
They shall be brought (and made) to drink poison and blood and defiled water and water from within the body; this shall be the drink of the heathen.

---

187. طرِكر *tsirkar*] should be درك *dirka*, cf. line 106.

189. ميامن *maiamimu*] according to Abd-el-Kadr is the name of a rock in hell.

190. The MS., which is somewhat indistinct, should read

مَتْيِذَى كُوَ سُيُو غَيَا غَرَنْسُ   سُفَرْ مَسْ سُوْ دَفِيّ سُكْ بُنْغُلَاوَا

فر *far*] is a Sokoto usage for فد *fada* "fight."

191. اكونا *akona*] "burnt," or we may read اكورا *akora* "driven away," cf. MS.

صعود *ṣa'uda*] Ar. "high," applied to the rock Maiaminu, line 189, note.

192. شكى اكنجن *shiki akanjan*] from *jan chiki* "to crawl."

Wuta kua gata ta yi fushi da ḳona   tana karya gabobin káfirawa
Asa masu sasari na wuta da malwa   wuta ta kiwuyisu da tsawutawa
Suna tsirkar jama'a alkáfirawa   suna kuka anamanáa gaẓawa
Malaiku su tsaida ẓugaẓuganta   su fura wuta suna kuma tsawutawa
Akaisu su hawa maiaminu don su shawo   ruan ẓafi fa hanji na ẓubuwa
Machizai kua su yiwo gaia garinsu   su far masu su deffi su ka bungulàwa
Akonasu akaisu hau ṣa'uda   fa dutsi ni ga aẓaba alkáfirawa
Fa rubda shiki akanjan káfirawa   ga kaifi nan shina deffa káfirawa
Dubu kua shekarya ba su kan iyaka   tsawon dutsin ṣa'uda babu wawa
Su komo marbika du ẓasu taka   fa kuma dagashan atsawuta káfirawa
Fa kaito su gangara shan ḳarḳashisa   shikin ẓafi wuta su ka gangarawa
Akaisu gari ḷari'u kaẓa da zakumu   da gislín abinshin káfirawa
Wa yuthḳi aiar min ma ṣadidin   dalili kua akan maitanbaiawa
Wuta ta chisu har ta shini hanta   kaẓa fufu da hanji na ẓubuwa
Wuta kowa na fita ga ido ga baki   da hanshi duk wuta na firfitowa
Akaisu su sha deffi da jini da boli   ruan hanji abinshan káfirawa

---

194. مربكا *marbika*] possibly from Ar. ربك *rabak* "to be confused."

195. قرقشس *ḳarḳashisa*] for قلقشس *ḳalḳashisa* "underneath it."

196. زكوم *zakumu*] is probably a mistake for زقّوم *zaḳḳum*; *az-zaḳḳum* is the name of a tree in hell, cf. Koran, Surah xxxvii. 60.

غسلين *gislín*] Ar. "putrid matter flowing from the lost."

197. The quotation is from Surah xiv. 19; for يثقى *yuthḳi* we should read يسقى *yusḳa* "he shall be given to drink," "He shall be given to drink of water which consists of the liquids exuding from wounds."

199. فرفتووا *firfitowa*] a strengthened form of *fitowa* "to come out."

F And the brokers who have made unjust profits shall have garments of fir put upon them, without doubt.

They shall have trousers of fire and turbans of fire; fire shall devour then there shall they continue.

And those who have made unjust profits shall there be made manifest; the shall come with it (i.e. their profit) by the power of the Almighty.

The verse "And he that defrauds," is a reason, if there be anyone wh asks for a reason.

And those who regard stealing as lawful are heathen; in the fire, as we under stand, shall they continue.

And the children of the fire, all of them shall continue in pain; there wil be no coming out, they shall remain for ever there.

The fire, I understand, shall change them so that they shall be burnt al over, they all shall become like charcoal, without doubt.

The Glorious One shall renew the fire, (and they shall be as a) new creation the fire shall destroy all the heathen.

And the verse "As often as they are roasted," is indeed the reason, if ther be anyone who asks.

They shall begin to cry out to the angels, they shall repent, (and say) Bring us again to the earth, we will follow the way of the Almighty.

It will be said to them, Remain in the pain; as for you, indeed, do y hear, (God) sent the prophets (to you).

And you (said), Who hath seen this, the next world, and hath returned? thi was the saying of you heathen.

And you said, There will be no resurrection nor pain; lament for yourselves ye heathen.

All the believers passing over the bridge shall come to the water of heaven without doubt.

They shall congratulate each other on having crossed the bridge withou fear on the part of any.

There shall be put on them beautiful garments of wool, and beautiful chain shall they hang (upon themselves).

---

201. دلالی *dallálai*] Ar. "brokers"; they act as intermediaries in the marke and receive from the seller 5 p.c. of the price arranged.

ماسربا *masuriba*] "those who make unlawful profits."

ماسكورا *masukura*] "those who keep back part of the money for the thing sold."

204. The quotation is from Surah iii. 155, "It is not for any prophet to defraud and whosoever defrauds shall produce his frauds on the day of the resurrection."

205. ماسحلل *masuhalal*] "those who regard as lawful," cf. Ar. حلال *halá* "lawful."

Fa dallálai fa masuriba da kura   asa masu riguna wuta babu wawa
Da wandunan wuta fa kaẓa rawuna   wuta na shinsu nan su ka tabettawa
Fa masuriba ashan akabayennasu   su ẓo su da shi da iko maiíyawa
Fa aiar shan waman yaglul dalili   dalili kua akan maitanbaiawa
Fa masuhalal ta gululu káfirai ni   chikin wuta mun ji shan su ka tabettawa
Fa yan wuta duk su duma shikin aẓaba   fa babu fita ashan su ka tabettawa
Jahími na ji ta maishisu ḳurmus   su juya kamar göi duk babu wawa
Fa jalla shi maida wuta sabon halita   wuta na karya jama'u alkáfirawa
Fa aiar kullama naḍijat hakika   dalili kua akan maitanbaiawa
Su dora kira fa malaiki su fa tuba   akaimu ga dúnia mu bi maiíyawa
Ashe masu kun ku duma shikin aẓaba   fa ai ku kun ji aiki annabawa
Fa ku ku she wa gano shi a lakhira nan   da ya komo fadar ku fa káfirawa
Fa ku ku she babu tashi ba aẓaba   ku kuka da kanku ya alkáfirawa
Jama'a al-muminai duka kan ṣirati   su kan tusga ta kauchara babu wawa
Suna barka da jiuna tsitariwa   ṣirati babu shakka ko ga kowa
Asa masu riguna na ado da mulufi   da siliyoyi ado su ḳa ratayawa

---

209. The quotation is from Surah iv. 59, "Behold those who have disbelieved in our signs, we will burn them with fire; as often as their skins are roasted we will give them new skins."

215. بركا *barka*] usually "to thank" or "to bless," cf. C 30, E 38, here means "to congratulate."

طتريوا *tsitariwa*] should apparently be كتريوا *kitariwa*, cf. MS., or better قتريوا *ḳitariwa* "crossing."

F They shall put on garments of silk, they shall rejoice with all the prophets.

And the verse "And he will reward them," is sufficient for you, if there be anyone who asks a reason.

They shall mount thus on camels and horses; there shall be golden saddles for everyone.

And the verse "We shall gather together," is sufficient for you, if there be anyone who asks a reason.

Mohammed, the messenger of God, has gone before them into heaven, the place of continuance.

And heaven shall be opened, (a place) of pleasure, they, together with Ridwanu, rejoice all of them.

They will say, Enter and remain where pleasure is, the abode of paradise, the place of continuance.

The verse "Therefore enter it," is sufficient for you, if there be anyone who asks a reason.

(Enter) into the rooms of gold and of silver; they shall put on also armlets, and that without doubt.

The verse "And they shall be made to wear armlets," is sufficient for you, if there be anyone who asks.

So too, there shall be rooms of ruby, of pearl, and of emerald, dost thou hear? in the place of continuance.

They shall marry Houris who grow not old; women shall be an object of regard to all.

And their faces shall be brighter than fire, there shall be seventy thousand women for each.

They shall drink wine and syrup made with honey, and soup; there shall be cooked food for all.

And Mohammed shall say, All ye believers, come, that ye may be brought into the dwelling-place of the Almighty.

---

218. The quotation is from Surah lxxvi. 12, "He will reward them......with paradise and silken robes."

For وجزيهم of text we should read وجزاهم.

219. سراد *suradi*] plural of سرد *surdi* "saddle," the more usual form is سردون *surduna*.

220. The quotation is from Surah xix. 88, "On the day when we gather together the pious to enter the presence of the Compassionate One."

222. انبوطى *anbutsi*] for انبودى *anbudi* "opened."

رضوان *riḍwanu*] Ar. "the name of the angel who stands at the door of heaven."

Su sa kuma rigunansu na alharini   suna murna da jamaʻu annabawa

Fa aiar wajazaḥum ta ishiku   dalili ko akan maitanbaiawa

Su hau kuma raḳuma ḥaka kua dawaki   suradi kua na zinaria ga kowa

Fa aiar shan wa nahshuru ta ishiku   dalili ko akan maitanbaiawa

Muhammadu er-rasulu shina gabbansu   ẓua aljenna dakin tabettawa

Fa anbutsi fa aljenna ta níma   su riḍwanu suna murna da kowa

Su she ku shigga ku tabetta enda níma   giddan aljennat dakin tabettawa

Fa aiar fadkhuluḥa ta ishiku   dalili ko akan maitanbaiawa

Ga dakin kua na zinaria azurfa   su sa kuma ḳundeggi kuma babu wawa

Wa hullu ai asawira ta ishiku   dalili ko akan maitanbaiawa

Kaẓa kuma dakunan yaḳutu murjan   zumurrud ka ji dakin tabettawa

Su amri fa huruʻaini da babu tsofa   fa matayi abin baḳi ga kowa

Fa fuskokinsu sun fi wuta da haski   dubu sabäin matayi ga kowa

Su sha gia du da madya ga zuma nan   ruan nama abin soiya ga kowa

Muhammadu kuma shi je jamaʻa almusulmi   ku ẓo en kaikú fa dar maiíyawa

---

223. سشي *su she*] "they will say," the true reading is يشي *ya she* "he will say."

224. The quotation is from Surah xxxix. 73, "And the guardian thereof shall say to them, Peace be upon you, ye are well pleasing, therefore enter it to abide for ever."

226. The quotation is from Surah lxxvi. 21, "They shall be made to wear armlets of silver." اي *ai* indeed does not form part of the quotation.

227. ياقوت *yaḳut*] Ar. "ruby, sapphire," or any precious stone.

زمرد *zumurrud*] Ar. "emerald."

228. ابن بقي *abin baḳi*] lit. "a thing regarded," cf. Ar. بقى *baḳá* "to regard" or "protect."

231. در *dar*] for Ar. دار *dár* "dwelling-place," so line 237.

F There shall be placed on them garments with the beauty of heaven, (each) different; there shall be joy and gladness for all.
Chains shall be bound on their right and left (hands), and silken sword-belts shall be bound on each.
They shall mount and gallop, clapping their hands together; they shall assemble to the house of the messenger (of God), who excels all.
The gate of our prophet, the son of Amina, shall be thronged, there shall be rejoicing with all the prophets.
Angels and messengers (shall be there); the gate of Mohammed, who excels all, shall be thronged.
After waiting for his coming out, they rise up and mount and go to the dwelling-place of the Almighty.
Mohammed, son of Amina, who excels all, prepares his garments, (which are an) object of adornment.
He mounts again upon his (horse) Buráka; they follow him, they go as an escort in front, in very truth.
They come to the place of Hasan; they praise Mohammed, who excels all.
There shall be a blowing of the heavenly flute, they shall go to the dwelling-place of the Almighty.
Abubekr shall be at the right hand of Mohammed, Omaru and Othman shall rejoice with everyone.
So too Ali, Telha, Zobeir, Saad and Saîd shall be on his right hand, without doubt.
So too the son of Awf and Amiru shall be there, and all the friends of Mohammed, and all the prophets.
And they all shall surround the son of Amina, they shall rejoice and go to (the place of) the Almighty.
They shall appear in the realm of the glorious King, our desire will obtain fulfilment.
Heaven and pleasure shall be forgotten, the sight of God surpasses them entirely.

---

232. شقا *shiga*] lit. a triangular piece of cloth inserted at the bottom of a robe, so as to make the bottom broader than the top, here apparently used for garments generally.

233. حميلو *hamilu*] Ar. حميلة *hamilat* "a sword belt," usually made of silk.

239. براكا *buráka*] for براق *burák*, the name of the horse on which Mohammed ascended to heaven.

240. حسان *hasanu*] according to Abd-el-Kadr this means "the place of Hasan." He was the son of Ali and noted for his great patience. The more correct form would be الحسان *al-hasanu*.

241. الغيت *algaito*] a wind instrument somewhat similar to a bag-pipe.

Adora shiga adon aljenna bamban	anafaraa anamurna da kowa
Adamri siliyu kuma dama hauni	hamilu duk ana kuma ratayawa
Adora suka da ban hanu da jiuna	ataru giddan rasulu da ya fi kowa
Fa anshika ḳofayan annabinmu dan amina	anamurna da jamaʿu annabawa
Malaiku kaẓa fa da mursalina	fa anshika ḳofara ahmadu ya fi kowa
Ana fa jiran fitowa nasa atashi	ahau kuma ẓatsa fa dar maiíyawa
Shiga sirin shiga kayan adonsa	muhammad tsan aminatu ya fi kowa
Shi hau kuma kan burāka tas abishi	su saʿdanu suna gabba babu wawa
Su hasanu suna kuma yin kirari	muhammadu er-rasulu da ya fi kowa
Ana kuma busa algaiton sarwata	amiḳa ẓua ga fa dar maiíyawa
Abubekri shina damshi muhammad	omaru othman suna murna da kowa
Kaẓa ai aliyu telhata har zubairu	da saʿdu saʿidu dama fa babu wawa
Kaẓa tsan oufu amiru ga shi nana	ṣahabani duk da jamaʿu annabawa
Fa duk ankiwoyi kowa dan amina	anamurna fa ẓatsa ga maiíyawa
Abayenna enda ẓatin jalla sarki	dada guri namu nan shi ka kua shikawa
Amanta kua da aljenna da níma	gani allaḥu ba shi abin gamawa

سروتا *sarwata*] probably intended for سموتا *samwata* "heavens," Ar. سموات *samawat.*

242. عمر *omaru*] Omar, a supporter of Mohammed, afterwards Khalif.

Mohammed's six principal adherents during the first three years were Ali son of Abu Taleb, Abu Bekr son of Abi Kohafa, Othman son of Affan, Abdelrahman son of Awf (cf. text), Saad son of Abi Wakkas, Zobeir son of Awwam, and Telha son of Obeidallah.

246. ددا *dada*] a Sokoto usage for كم *kuma* "again." Perhaps this is the sense in which it is used in C 21.

247. ابن غماوا *abin gamawa*] lit. "a thing to come up to or to equal."

F And the verse "Their faces..." is sufficient for you, if there be anyone wh asks a reason.
They shall return again to heaven and remain thus for ever; there shall b no death for any.
O God, place us amongst the people of Mohammed, our prophet, wh excels all.
That I may go forth from Sokoto is my desire, to Medina, where i Mohammed, who excels all.
In the house of the son of Bazo would I stay; and indeed I fear m parents in very truth.
And it is because I fear my parents that I do not go to the city c Mohammed, who excels all.
And I myself, do ye hear, make this song of instruction; my own life i indeed my friend.
Ye men of Kano, I make this song of instruction in the twelve hundre and sixtieth year of the Hegira.
I have finished this song and render thanks to God, and greetings be wit Mohammed, who excels all.

With the praise of God (is this song) completed, and good success and prais be to God, the Lord of the worlds.

---

248. وُجُوهُمْ *wujuhum*] this form does not occur in the Koran. We shoul perhaps read وجوهٌ *wujuhun* "faces"; the quotation would then be from Sura lxxv. 22, "On that day shall faces beam with light outlooking towards their Lord.

250. جماعر *jama'ar*] for جمع *jama'u*, cf. line 244.

251. i.e. the tomb of Mohammed, which is at Medina.

252. Bazo was a famous Mallam who lived in Kano.

253. The argument apparently is that respect for his parents, and his u willingness to desert them, is the reason for his failure to go on the pilgrimage.

Fa aiar shan wujuḥum ta ishiku   dalili ko akan maitanbaiawa
Akomo kuma ga aljenna aduma   tutur haka babu mutua kua ga kowa
Fa ya allaḥu ka samu chikin jama'ar   muhammadu annabinmu da ya fi kowa
Da na fita sokoto kua ni nuffina   madinatu enda ahmada ya fi kowa
Giddan kua dan bazo anasoka ni kua   da kua soron iyayi babu wawa
Fa ba domin ina tsoron iyayi   fa da na je ga ahmada ya fi kowa
Fa raina kun ji na yiwa wonga waatsi   abokina fa raina babu wawa
Kanawa fa na yi waḳa nana waatsi   nurayishu ramzu ḥijra babu wawa
Fa na gama waḳa na godia allaḥ   ṣalatu ya duma ga ahmada ya fi kowa

Tammat bihamd allaḥi wa husn 'auniḥi wa-l-hamd li-llaḥi rabb al-'álamína

---

254. The meaning of the latter half of this line is uncertain, perhaps it should be "I indeed, myself, O my friend."

255. نريش *nurayishu*] the consonants of this word make up the number 1260: ن = 50, ر = 200, ي = 10, ش = 1000. The 1260th year of the Hegira would be A.D. 1843.

This would represent the date of its reduction to writing by Abdallah, cf. introduction to F.

رمز *ramzu*] an Arabic word (*ramaz*) sometimes used to denote unity.

HISTORY OF ZARIA.

G 1 In the name of God, the Compassionate, the Merciful, and of Him do we ask help.

The book of the history of the kings of Zaria from Mallam Musa, a Beriberi, until the time of Othman, we are about to give you.

The history (we give) by the help of God. Mallam Musa, then, obtained the kingdom of Zaria; he came and made war against the people of Zaria, he drove them away, they set forth, they went, they came to Mangi, they remained (there). He prepared to start, he followed them as far as Mangi, and when they heard of his movements, they rose up, they went to the land of Guri; they made a city there, it was called Habuja, they settled down in it;
G 2 after this he rose up || he went to the south to a certain land called the land of Umüaisha, he fought with its people; he destroyed them, he burnt the town, he came to the town of Zozo with thirteen hundred slaves; he came with (many) horses, he rose up, he went to war with a certain country called Kugama; (the people of that country) caused him loss; there was slain Kakumi a certain warrior whom he loved, he lamented, he rose up and returned to Zaria, he made preparations, he went to their town, he conquered them, he returned and remained in Zaria, he made war eight times, he remained at home nine years, he died in Zaria. After the death of Mallam Musa, the Beriberi, Yamusa a native of Mali obtained the kingdom of Zaria; he made war once, he did not obtain the victory, he lived three years in the kingdom of Zaria, he died. After Yamusa, Abdalkarími obtained the

---

The following history of Zaria is an extract from a much longer history written in Arabic. It was translated into Hausa at my request by a Mallam in Zaria. The history covers the period from the deposition of the Hausa kings and the establishment of the Fulahs in their place down to the present time. From the time of Musa, the first of the Fulah dynasty, twelve kings in all have reigned in Zaria. The state of Zaria includes all the country lying to the south of the town as far as the river Binue. At the time of the Fulah usurpation of the kingdom a large number of the pagan Hausas retreated towards the mountainous districts south of the town, where they succeeded in maintaining their independence. The town of Zaria contains a population of about thirty thousand and is itself tributary to Sokoto.

G 1. نستعين *nasta'înu*] "we ask for help," X. form of Ar. عون *'an*.

HISTORY OF ZARIA.

1 Bismi allaḥi errahmáni errahími wa biḥi nasta'ínu

Litáfi na labári sarakuna ẓariar dagga malamu musai babarbari har ya ẓua
ẓamani othmanu shi ẓamu baku labári da iko allaḥ amma malam musai ya chi
sarota ẓaria da ya ẓo ya yi yaki da mutanen ẓaria ya koresu suka fita suka
taffi suka je mangi suka ẓamna ya saki tashi ya bisu har mangi da ka ji
mutsinshi suka tashi suka taffi ḳasa guri su kan gari anache mashi habuja
2 suka ẓamna chiki baya wonan ya tashi || ya taffi kudu ga wani kasa anakiran
ḳasa umüaisha ya yi fatsa da su ya ḥalakasu ya ḳona gari ya ẓo gari na ẓoẓo
da bayi dubu da tsari uku ya ẓo da dawaki ya saki tashi ,ya taffi yaki wani
kasa sunanshi kugama su kai mashi berna anan akakasshi kakumi wani maiyaki
da ya ki sonshi ya yi kuka ya tashi ya komo ẓaria ya saki shiri ya taffi
garisu ya chisu ya komo ya ẓamna chikin ẓaria ya yaki tokkos ya ẓamna abin-
shi shekara shi tara ya mutu chikin ẓaria bayan mutua malam musa babarbari
yamusa bamali ya chi sarota ẓaria ya yi yaki so tsaia bai yi naṣara ba ya
shekara uku chiki sarota ẓaria ya mutu baya yamusa abd-al-karími ya chi

---

ببربري *babarbari*] usually pronounced Beriberi, a name applied to the inhabitants of Bornu. The Fulahs who conquered Zaria had long been resident in Bornu near Lake Chad, and are distinct from the Fulahs of Sokoto.

موطنش *mutsinshi*] "his movement." In the province of Zaria ش *shi* is frequently used as a suffix instead of س *sa* "his."

G 2. ذذوا *ẓoẓo*] another name for Zaria, it is also sometimes called Zegzeg.

ابنش *abinshi*] lit. "his affair," here equivalent to "by himself." ابنك *abinka* is used similarly.

بملي *bamali*] "native of Mali." Mali is the name of a town near Ilorin in the Yoruba country.

G 3 kingdom of Zaria, || he (continued) nine years, he rose up, he went to Chori,
he made war with the people, he conquered them, he prepared to start, he
went to war with Jaba, he conquered its people; the king of Jaba was
captured, he was killed there, he returned to Zaria, he remained two years,
after this he prepared to set out, he went to war with Gwari, he conquered
it, he returned, he remained nine years, he died. After the death of Abdal-
karími, Mohamma Chani, a Beriberi, obtained the kingdom of Zaria; he rose
up, he went to war with Gitata in the west, he did not conquer its people,
he returned, he waited, he prepared to start, he returned to it but did not
conquer its people, he returned, he remained in Zaria, he went against
Gitata twelve times, then he called upon God, the Lord, then he conquered
its people. After fighting against and capturing Gitata he returned, he
G 4 started again, he went || northwards to Sokoto, he did not like to fight, he
went away. In this war was killed a great man who was called the Madaki,
he lamented much, he returned thence to Zaria, he continued in his kingdom
nine years; the wars (that he waged were) four. After his death Sidi Ba-Mali
obtained the kingdom of Zaria; after he had obtained it he said, Except
with oil no one shall enter with anything tied up into the town of Zaria,
on pain of being killed; thus did he reign, killing very many men, he made
war twice, he rose up and went to Sokoto, he was driven out from his
kingdom. After his expulsion Sidi Hamada obtained the kingdom of Zaria,
his days were fifty-three, he died, he made no war; in his reign there
was security of land for all men, you might travel (in safety), alone, to the
East, West, South, and North, nothing would happen to you. After the
reign of Hamada, Abdalsalámi made himself king of Zaria; he moreover ||
G 5 went to war with Kauru, he was shot by an arrow, he died, he returned
not, (he reigned) nine months. After king Abdalsalámi Abdu made himself
king of Zaria, he lived fourteen years in his kingdom; at the beginning
of his reign he rose up, he went to war with Gunu, he did not conquer
its people, he returned, he waited, he prepared to start, he went forth
to war with the family of Diko, a great man amongst the heathen, he
conquered him; Diko was captured, he went with him in front of him, he
(Diko) was killed; after this war he rose up and went to the gate of Kaffi,

---

G 3. غورى *gwari*] usually called Birnin-Gwari, a large town about fifty miles west of Zaria, now within the territory of the king of Kwontagora.

غتاتا *gitata*] Gitata, which repelled the attack of the king of Zaria twelve times, is about 100 miles south-west of Zaria. It is situated on a very steep rocky incline, and owing to the strength of its position is still semi-independent. For description of this district cf. *Hausaland*, p. 66.

G 4. اككشى *akakachi*] for اككش *akakashi* "was killed."

ماداكى *madaki*] "chamberlain," a title applied to one of the chief officials in

3 sarota ẓaria || shekaranshi tara ya tashi ya taffi chori ya yi yaki da su ya chisu
ya saki tashi ya taffi yaki ajaba ya chisu akakama sarki jaba akayenkasshi
dagana ya komo ẓaria ya ẓamna shikara biu bayasa ya saki fita ya taffi yaki
agwari ya chisa ya komo ya ẓamna shekara shi tara ya mutu baya mutua
abd-al-karími mahamma chani babarbari ya chi sarota ẓaria ya tashi ya taffi
yaki agitata ayamma bai chisu ba ya komo ya ẓamna ya saki tashi ya koma
bai chisu ba ya komo ya ẓamna ẓaria aẓuanshi goma sha biu agitata saanan
ya roki ubangíji allaḥ ya chisu saanan baya yaki gitata da ya chisu ya kuma
4 tashi ya taffi || ariwa asakoto bai son anayaki ba ya taffi anan chiki yaki
akakachi da shi baba anache mashi madaki ya yi kuka maiyawa dagana ya
komo ẓaria ya ẓamna chiki sarotashi shekarashi tara yakinshi fudu baya
mutuashi sidi bamali ya chi sarota ẓaria da ya chi ya che banda da mai ba
ashiggo da komi atsamri abirni ẓaria sai shi ya kasshi hakanan ya yi ẓamanishi
sai shi ta yenka mutane yaki da ya yi so biu ya tashi ya taffi sakoto akafita
da shi achiki sarotashi baya fito sidi hamada ya chi sarota ẓaria kwananshi
khamsin da uku chiki sarota ya mutu ba yi yaki ba amutanen duka achiki
zamanishi da kasa amána ni sai ka yi taffía kai tsaia gabbas da yamma da
kudu da ariwa ba abinda ẓai sameka baya sarota hamada abd-al-salámi ya yi
5 sarki ẓaria shi kua || ya taffi yaki akoro akahalbeshi da kibia ya mutu bai
komo ba watashi tara baya sarki abd-al-salámi abdu ya yi sarki ẓaria yai
shekara goma sha fudu achikin sarota far kua sarotashi ya tashi ya taffi yaki
agunu bai chisu ba ya komo ya ẓamna ya saki tashi ya taffi yaki giddan diko
wani babba káfiri ya chishi akakamu diko akaẓua da shi gabbanshi akayen-
kashi baya wanan yaki ya tashi ya taffi kofan kaffi ya yi yaki da kaffi ya

---

several of the Hausa States. The order of precedence at Zaria is sariki, madaki, galladima, sarikin makira, etc.

بند *banda*] more commonly written بمد *bamda* "besides."

شي تينكا *shi ta yenka*] apparently a mistake for شي يينكا *shi ya yenka*.

امان *amána*] Ar. *amán* "security." For other meaning of *amána* cf. E 15, 25.

G 5. كفى *kaffi*] Kaffi, a town of about 20,000 inhabitants, 160 miles south of Zaria, to which it is now tributary.

he made war with Kaffi, he returned, he waited, he prepared to start again,
he went to Warji to make war with it, together with Abdallahi, the king
of Kano, they conquered its people; after this war he made four wars, he
(continued) fourteen years in his kingdom, he was then driven out. After
the expulsion of the king Abdu, Abubekr obtained the kingdom of Zaria, he
G 6 rose up and went to war with Guddo, || he conquered its people, his time was
two years and five months, and he died. After the death of Abubekr, Abdu
returned to the kingdom, his time was five years and five months, he was
then expelled (again); after the departure of Abdu, Sanbo obtained the
kingdom of Zaria, he rose up and went to war with Libiri, he conquered its
people, he returned and waited, he prepared to start again, he went to
Kachachari, he conquered its people, he returned and waited, he prepared to
start again, he went to war with Fiti, he did not conquer its people, he
returned, he waited, he prepared to start again, he went to war the fourth
time with Isa, he did not conquer its people, he returned, he waited in his
kingdom, his time was nine years and six months, he was driven out of his
kingdom. Ba Sanbo, his time was eight years and six months; on a Thursday
the Anbutawa came to Zaria to make war, they killed many of the people
of Zaria (during) the reign of Chanbo. After the departure of Sanbo, Othman
G 7 obtained the kingdom || of Zaria, he (lived) five months in the kingdom, he
rose up, he went to war with Fiti, he conquered its people, he burnt this
town and he returned, he waited, he prepared to start (again), he went
to Rukuba, he made war with its people, he did not conquer them, he
returned, he waited, he prepared to start (again), he went to Kufana, he
did not conquer its people, he returned, he waited, he prepared to start
(again), he went to Dakolo, he conquered its people, he returned, he waited,
he prepared to start again, he went to war with Kuchinda, he conquered its
people, he returned, he waited, he rose up, he went to war with Abuja, he
returned not, he conquered them not, this was his sixth war.

This is the account of the kings of Zaria, twelve in number, from Mallam Musa the Beriberi to Othman, who is now king, and of the wars which they waged. This account is reliable. The account is completed by the will of God. It is finished.

G 6. كششرى *kachachari*] probably to be identified with Kachia, a town about 90 miles south of Zaria, between it and Kaffi.

با سنب *ba sanbo*] i.e. the son of Sanbo.

ثنب *chanbo*] apparently a mistake for سنب *sanbo*.

komo ya ẓamna ya saki tashi ya taffi warji garin yaki da shi da sarkin kano
abd-al-laḥi suka chisu baya wanan yaki ya saki yaki fudu ya shekara goma
sha fudu chikin sarota akafisheshi baya fito sarki abdu abubekr ya chi sarota
6 ẓaria ya tashi ya taffi yaki aguddo || ya chisu shekarashi biu da wata biar ya
mutu baya mutu abubekr abdu ya komo chikin sarota shekarashi biar da wata
biar akafishishi baya fito abdu sanbo ya chi sarota ẓaria ya tashi ya taffi yaki
alibiri ya chisu ya komo ya ẓamna ya saki tashi ya taffi kachachari ya chisu
ya komo ya ẓamna ya saki tashi ya taffi yaki afiti bai chisu ba ya komo ya
ẓamna ya saki tashi ya taffi yaki na fudu äisa bai chisu ba ya komo ya ẓamna
chiki sarota nasa shekarashi tara da wata shidda akafita da shi asarotashi ba
sanbo shina da shekara tokkos da wata shidda rana al-khamis anbutawa suka
ẓo aẓaria garin yaki suka kasshi mutane ẓaria dayawa chikin sarota sarki
7 chanbo baya fita da sanbo othman ya chi sarota || ẓaria shina da wata biar
achikin sarota ya tashi ya taffi yaki afiti ya chisu ya kona garina da ya komo
ya ẓamna ya saki tashi ya taffi rukuba ya yi yaki da su bai chisu ba ya komo
ya ẓamna ya saki tashi ya taffi kofana bai chisu ba ya komo ya ẓamna ya saki
tashi ya taffi dakolo ya chisu ya komo ya ẓamna ya saki tashi ya taffi yaki
akuchinda ya chisu ya komo ya ẓamna ya tashi ya taffi yaki abuja bai komo
ba bai chisu ba yakinshi shidda

wanan labári sarakuna ẓaria su goma sha biu tunda ga malam musa babarbari har ya ẓua othman na yanẓu da yakoki da suka yi wanan labári ankatashi ni wanan litáfi ta chika bisa yerda allaḥ tammat.

Throughout this extract ط, which elsewhere denotes *ts*, is employed to denote the sound *d*. Thus *tsari* is written for *dari*, *tsaia* for *daia*. For the sake of uniformity I have retained the former transliteration, but the ط should be pronounced as *d*.

HAUSA CHARM.

The directions for using this charm are as follows: a facsimile of this is to be written out on a smooth piece of board, the ink used is then to be washed off and the mixture of water and ink so obtained is to be drunk, the result being, if the native belief be correct, that any person whom the drinker of the mixture has in his mind at the time, will thenceforth conceive an affection for him. Every Hausa native who has been to Mecca is believed to have acquired the power of writing charms of this kind, which are capable of causing or curing disease, and of injuring or benefiting any given person. An additional degree of sanctity and therefore of power in regard to charm-writing is supposed to attach to a man who has made the pilgrimage more than once.

The signs in the small squares are not letters and have no signification by themselves.

LIST OF WORDS REFERRED TO IN THE NOTES.

CAMBRIDGE: PRINTED BY J. AND C. F. CLAY, AT THE UNIVERSITY PRESS.

FACSIMILES

A. بسم الله الرحمن الرحيم وصلى الله على من لا نبي بعده

بسم نا قلرا الله ييردن ميسهل كي تيمكوا غرين ذشتكر

(3) (4) ذرنش خيام باب ميتكا ادشا سي كوكتبى كحى غمز غذو مى نعوكر

(5) تحو كي ي اقوا اناد ذ نحو وجم وعلم كل مسلم بلر وا الكافر

شي ني شيكنج جدا انبا ي كنوا سي دي شتاد حبا ايجا اكبر برا

شي ني شيجي شك تمزاب الاخرا سي يا غمود وتا يكبتي كنزا

مالي كدع نحو سر وتاد وكيا زانا غمود ملاحكو نحس دير ي

ونريحر ا تو حمزبن ذكني مسا سوسهو د بشي شيكر الكامري

(10) اتاد و نيشنا ابن منو مه الاخرا كو وا اينو مو قطي يكيبس نمزه

اتبن د ساجي تكنحد مكر ريغ نا ونذو امينا في مم اينه توبرا

كمي وكزو تاد كشاد ادشا نكا مي كفر بنا كاج وار اغنفر

(13) اتاد و نيشتاد كمل ذكر تكم دامغ ازكعر اعم بلاج ي زر

اتادني

a

اناد ونى ننا كلو فواكى كتتى سنه كلو بوا بير كيبا هاتى آبو بكر A

اناد ونينا كوسونى كر سنه كوا ايه و يسونى كبا كوكر يمر

شوشى كرا نو شى كى ذ الاخر سيدى عمد اديطو ق كلو جو هبير

الز اكبر قينا سعفو كجر قينا كدد ركتار حنو ى كر كلور بر

ات دو ينسر بت مسوم الاخر جمع منس عمزر شغ بب عمر

ور كرانو حمز بن محمد شنسسو نجركر شنب ود بجنالر

سونر مغاد آنبا وا امالقى واجب مرو قيس وند بجى عمر

شر سر مر سنسس بكر دك شر جمل ا بك كا شكى ار كر نعم مالقى

د ربو وتا نام بكم نس كتجى شنسسو نجركر شنب و نو نعمبر

انش شكنا طمك عمد نس سنا كلر كدد نسبر مات سيا و ثكر عمر

نو ملاغم ما تنابى كمات بكر سنى كن برغم ادنى كر كمسا تنا اكنكر

مات دكر شنا نبغ نعبيا اك دغ كوسو فر غن بكر دوك زور

بكن باك يارو ذيدو نولو نتا بك كو كر ركر روا اثكر درب

كو دا يمد نش نكر سوات تنبيا كبا تنا يرج سر تمرا اثكر در

A

قَدِرِ وُنِي تَرُضِي اَجِكِي تَنَا ، تَجِبِكِتُ حَرِ مَعَنَا اَجِبِتُ اَنَبِرُنِ

اُنسُو تُكِشِ هُرِ بِرِنْكِرِ مغِ نَا اَنَنَا كَدِ ذَرِ اَجِبِنْ سَا عُمُرِ وَكِرِ كِرَا

كَاْرِ بِكِنْفِي دِكِي اَلْفُوَرِ بِكِي تَنِي كُوَ مَنَا كِي سِرِ دُدُمُ عَزِرِ

مَا اَتَ دِ كِي تِعِيَا دِكِي تَنَا جِبِلَرِ جُو رَانَا فِيَامَ كَرُو تَنَا تَ بِ كِي

مَا اَتَ دِكِي تِعِيَا دِكِي تَنَا بَارِجُو رَانَا فِيَامَ تَارِ فُوَا بُرِ عُوَا وُتَنَا

اُمُسَ مُتُمْ بِيُو سُسِ تَسَا الآخِرَ آرَانِ فِيَامِ دُسِ تَنَا اِيشِ كُمُرِ كِرِى

وَ تَنِ دِكِي كُنِ مَا الِمِ دِ جَدَ انُسَا سَنِينِي يِكِي غَا اِبُ دَا اِنِي كَا اُ بِرِ

وَتِنِ دِكِي اَذُمُو اَبُوتِي شَكَرَ تَبَا نِي بَابُ نَا اَشَكِ كُنِي مُسِ كَا اِبِرِ

يِمَنَ دُ وُنِيَا تَنِي مُسُومِ الآخِرَا جَمْعَا اُمُسِ عُذُرِ نَشَكَا اِبِرِ عُمْرِ

كُووُ بِكِي رُتُو تِبَا اُمُرِ نَا اَنَنَا تَنِينِي بِبِسُو دِعُذُرِ وُتَلَاحِ رِ بِمُرِدِهَا

كُووُ تِيبِسُودِ عُذُرِ وُتَلَاحِرِ بِمُرِدِهَا يَا اَتَرِدِ تُوُ تَا وُنِدِ بَاتِ مَعَكُرَا

كُوَ اِيدَاتِ يَا كِ ذَابِ الآخِرَا نَنِينِي بِ وِكِ وُرِي بِبِرِ تُو يَادِرِ

اللهُ تَعَلَى يَا اِنِ بِبِوَا اَهِي بِوَا اَعُذُ بِفِيَامِ سَنِ مُتُمُ الصَّابِرِ .

اَتَكِي

A.

انكو دره دِيا كبرتَ ادونِيا   نعشعين نشا نن ياكفرا دمما انز

مِت مادين دامنا بنى كمنسنى   نسعين نشا بن الاخرا دمما انز

مت بنى دليل سا اموام ندونيا   نكوو ابنشيس نعلم هبر الاخرا

نكومِ كبا بزكا شبنش الاخرا   اجير دبا بيرر بكى توسر نخرا

نكا انا امش عكبى نشور الاخرى   نكومِ مسكجسو سى شغنش انبرى

تونر دكى صدقا دبيسوا اكى بوا   سى مرصلا مى عبادا ادرى

نبيوسر و ند نبلا ابا و درجا   درك زمنغ نيفوا انكى عمرة

نفكنس و ند نعيش نوحيد كا   كومِ نسا امش سى بنش ربا الورى

نسركِ عند بار ابكونى الاخرى   سيكوا نوبا دا ابيشا الكوثرى

تسركِ نجر ما بنى د هالاعزة دكا   از بابا نو بابا بش الكوثرى

بابرى مسنى با بنصا بى سود كا   از بنى كنا سبا احد اس نكر و تا

نكا انا امش عكج نسكور الاخرا   سيكود نو با د اسشا الكوثرا

A.

وَنَدِ بِي صَلَا عَمَا جِنبَا رِدِ كُمْ بَابَ تُو بَاكُو عَمَا يِشِ دِكَاوِيرِ

وَنَرِ بِجِنْ رِكِ تِبِيهِمْرَ وَفِيتِي دِكَا كُمْ بَابَ تُجَا اِنجَا اِتِي مَسْ كَاوِيرِ

55 نَعُكُرُسُ وَ نَدَ بِيعِيشِ لَبِ جِرِسُوِ دِكَا وَفَرِ دِكُمْرِجِ بِينِزِ نَالَا اِنكِ عُزِرِ

كُمْ بَابُ كَمْرِجِي بَابَ صَلَا كُنِسِنِي كُمْ بَابَ مَالَا بَابُ تَشِ اَلْكَوْثَرَا

اِمَّا بَعْدُ تَنَا بَابُ تُو نَدَ سُكَرَا تَنَتَا مُكَوَا يِكِيتِ جُبَرِيشِ يَدَاخِمْ كَاوِرِ

اَثِكِرِ غَدِرِ الْجَنَّةِ بَابَا مُشِرِ عِمَكِ شِيبَا دَ صَفِيهَا سِبُ وَتُو بِغَنبَرِ

وَنَدِ كُوِر طَوَاوُ شِعَارِ دَ صَفِيهَا اَبِسَا مُكُنِشِ مِبِغِيَاوَا اَفَاوِرِ

60 بِيِسِ شِيِي عِمَى وَ نَدَ بَابَ عِمْبَا نَسِ شِينِي عُو نَتْسِتَارِ وَ نَدَ بِعَنْبَرِ

نَعُكُنِسِ وَنَدَ بِيعِيشِ لَبِنِ بِرِسُوِ دِكَا يِشِي يَادِ صَلَا وَ فِيِ نِتِ سُو بِيرِو

كُوَا اِيهِر تُو تُوَا بِشُو دِرِ يَابِتَا سِبِكُوَا دِ جَا وَ نَدِكِ عُنِ ظَاهِرِ

كُمْ بَارُ وَ الشِّ كُوِ دَ نُوتُ تَلِيمِ بُوَا رِشِ كُوِ جِبَ تِبِيقَمْرَ اَلِشِ عُزِرِ .

64 رِسِ كِدَ نُوتُو لِتَجِبِي يَسِفَلْمَكِ تُوتُو جِيكِرِ صَلَا جِبِرِ بِتِهَمْدِرِي

الله

b

A. 65 الله يكن عمر ازر فينك ذ جزبا آيسا بزي نو توا ينشو

دي طاهر

رانة زبقتو بكرونا كشنا معقا تكنا كشنروا كو بيشا كو غم بيز

زنز كشاق ذ عجوا كجر مر كشكا شعا كنا يكمشنا فيزنش كعمر دي

كلزكي عمق صلا كسن واجب يكي ذذ واجكنس دوا تجنس ذاو

قبز ضي غصلا غو مزني ذ عدا تكش سناذ كزيو منج سنجوشا بيز

70 مشنجبزة موم كسنس در كوزسعو كوا بيشا مسريا وكو قسرو

واجب كشنبي الوضنك كجسنا عنبي تبركر دكو بيزتد بيا

آيبزك وجب بني ذ بار كدو كنا آيسا جون كبرم الله اكبر

اما تكتبني ذ بار آبني وابعا كدو دي كرا كا تكشنكشنيني غرا

74 كوا ايكو بزر كرا شو وابعا بشبني يكرن كجماعة وكجميعر

A.

كووي بجو صلا يشا كن قلانجا يشيني ييكو ذ مكن جري بنسا باذري

نتبو كمسابي كككنا سوكن يمنى كمر بار ورا كابي كمسنك بيتش كري

ونن دكو شنكا ذنا رش الا اضرا ييتا ظو كلتيه الي اكس دبيكو جرا

زاناذ ميتبو سا بيوس كجو نسا زركيكو غ منتم عكس دبكرزبا

زاناذ ميتبو سا بيوس كجونسا زاركيكو غ منتم اكس د بيكو قنا

زنتو ككلو فا نو تعسا سكن ابنسا بصابي ونه يذم كا بري

كوا يلم ان ذكي تانه ينا عذوا ككنا عبا نس نا ب شا بنيبر

مابرك سام ذو وكيا ابكينسا اي بالك سام ذو وكيا اي ابو بكر

يشيني يتسا متاذك بملك النبي صوفا لم بيوذو بيي الفاجري

امي عمرة مكاث با و كن نكا بتش كم عزكن تكمبا ذو كري

ي كنتر تلي دكاي كتا ندو يا سوزاكجي كا ابشا الا اضرا

B.

بسم الله فر كور كلمات الله اكبر سبحان الله ١

الله لا اله الا الله محمد رسول الله فمنا ١

جبار واحد سركي الله عمر غمنم مو يوم مر غوبر ١

الله عمر عجمم نكر روفو كوم نكر بداد بكاتاتا ١

الله شطر كبر مم ايكم شبام حنفي د بصير اتس ١

الله عمر عجي كجفر باو ا باد ر ابند د اش شعيكابا ١

ار د ر ابر د د شعيكابر مبيبي بر غبر يد او وشبا ١

الله شطر كبر مر ايكنم شساشر صالحي بامو غوبا ١

الله عمر عجي شجفر باو ا شباري النبينسر شي تنو ١

مثبي بشر ربر عيابا سر يا قبر ابند كنو نا مر ١

ار باري تنبيا بر ابكابا شيكر د المخفينسر ر غوبس ١

تو تد باهي كنو اكيبر كو غو بر ابيت د ربشر ١

شي باهي شكر كماحوكا شي مكير شر باد عمر تو كا ١

د باهي شكر د وكا بيس غبا اشنا طنر الكا كيبر ١

كو ير غوا كفو اوط مالهي كنم شي ككور فالتو تلا

B.

كب محمد كسكتبر ا م كباد فو قرندك غسنا نشو م

انب ماغني بايا جيتا محمد ندنك باشر زغر نتو نتا م م

كونغنك ياغ ربوغو بو م ياطير بار فو با بنبيني م م

ضينك منب الله مر بهرد اامر ياد غسكياد آمنتشم م

مر دو غر بك فنا فمنا م الير كثنك سيد قسم نشو م

انا بيو بك سيد بمبر زهر ا م مجر حد بجر مز بو م مز غو بك م

كو بز غمو اكجير كسو زار ا م اكبر بو ند م مجر كلمانتا م

مز باد بياس غقو فظ م سوذا نبينا هك د نغينام

كووا قد فنس امير نزم ان فنبقد م شذا ب مر ادبني م

شيد وغد اغدا اتا طير بمو د و مر بغر غما سر اتا ربا م

غوا دياد بيس ككاز ابا م كاسر بكا غما سركا مر بنا م

تكو دو نبا د غمو نقو بر م كاسر بكا غما سركر فطبنا م

دو بااسري سحري كبيو دوبام تكنس كوبو ككد دابا م

شي وندكو بد رالبند تشر م كنسر بيشي كلات د دنيابام

شي وندكو جبر كبكي د ر غم م كنسر بشي كلاانا دلو هام

هكو لير عوا

c

B.

كواير غوالنيما افصلو لا ار كور فسر سو مك ابفاني لا

ابند تنفلي بو غلنبا لا لقا فاعد واسكا غنشر فرقو فرلا

ابند تنفلي كبر غا ابنوا لا كر سر عد و امشي غشر جذ ابا لا

بوند نفلي مبصيرا انترا لا سكر فر كبر شر مكا ابو بن لا

كدوب باطني نما يكنك لا ار سوري غا افنبا مو كيو كشغا لا

كوبر اكجفر جهاد يدن لا كبيد كنكر امبر نصا يوا لا

كيا و ذنبا كبر نصا بوا لا اكلمشن تولد بي غجكر لا

شي ونة دنيا اتر نجاي لا اشفو شر كر فتنا كها الو بر لا

كوبر غوا امنو با مبر صا بوا الا ار فنكيا بموغ دكيا اقمحي بالا

كودر غيو شنيم دغيكا و الا قد فتنكشر هنا بنا لا

ابند ما اولنك ينو نا ما الا ر فنشر كدكو ور دغيكين لا

كينا انكرني ياكو ور با لا دو مر نكنقد بر غيكا با لا

شي وند ير شن بر غيك با ما انا ابند ذا اشفد غو بر لا

كوبر غوا اكلا ركتي امسر لا ذر ذا ار ادغا امر ا انفاني لا

الله تشبا لم كلر كي كونركي لا يشبا لم كي دنشا ذابر يلم لا

B.

الله شقيلم كونالا قاقا د ببابو رازنى باليبينى

يقودنى دستادابر بينوا دلا قيبا عباداكر بادو

ارذ رندونيا ميكا روا بناى اد علا رشاقبا

دومرطولند ماقمواد يند نزونيا بناىر مرادييا

كوبر غوا اكبر تشغير دنيا كوو ئتا بابئسر عباديا

كستر دونيك مهابنك هستر لاحر نكمبر غوسة

كوويا دونيكبر بارود شنادونيا دابر ووروقى

كيذر ابوك كوركنا القرا كيمنفلر ابرد ككا ايكا

ارلحا شرووكبتر ربى بشينى ككا انتا ابرد ككر طوزو

مناد بقيا باقا ساوا ارككر شرا ابر بجشترياءبا

بل انكر درى كوكوديووقو كوكود ساقو تاساوا العمنطى

آيند كر كربا كركبا كهشر زنك كند شرابيبك

دوفرد زند زات ترابيكى نصارنزر ترتبر ككتا كنتر

نبذ مهيشنك نكر توس مد ذلمى عمر نك دبلبينى

بذارو عنا غنك ابر توس ككتا ندو نيبا بكبكا ابرا

دو با سرى

B.

دوباسر نسر ككم دنيا ه رود غمرت باتت دمانت ا
غد ندبا نطو ابلحو ناوا ه بلا افيا نكيت سي نو ننا ا
كوم ند ونيا هن فا رلوا ه ني بنغ ونغ ند اشر شدو ربنا ا
كيدن اسو فر ديو نفوير ه ابه دكنه غور كنز شكا ا
لكا اسر فنم بشر سر غور بنا ه اِن ذاكيم كبيشر نكر نور ا
الله كبر انشك غور بينا ه انجر فد برا ندمذ نغشكر ا
كوم لكر بعد ابكا نلكا ه روو نمجم بمبر نمجي بكتا ابا ا
الله نبسغ نمنم ابر فقنا ه شبا كي ينذ واغو بشفا رمها ا
كوم بمبر نمجي يا ابا اوا ه بامر رمي برلي مر فو نور ا
كو بر غوا كنور شيطان ه سنا كر سنيمك يشو شو شقر ا
كوم يفار زناشر شفا ربني ه فر فوم دونيا دك فا رلو ا
نادو ود ونيا هن با بنت ه نغ تنغ نلنكي بجبا دابا ا
د ادن انا دها دنيا دنكم ه دا النبي مدا انكي ذمسني ا
دكر د دونيا كوفاري دك ه دد وكيك دك دسر نلكا ا
انا ابرا اباكي دكا كنغ ه دد كسنو بش اكما البسذ منا با ا

B.

دوباغمبا ادرمنكبن وابرتاشنرسررنسودن

بياملكت بزرغرفوبيا شناكراد الحي بينغ غشكر

دوب فمرگمو فرودسرونياش دونباغباوكوكويابيارى

اى كاغ شركما ابسذ منابا ادونيادسورسرونشر

مزوبارواددبيرفاربا فباثرذكونكسرفارنوى

شى وندار كوشرد فرزوا فافارشبزنكا نشكر سرفرنوى

كوابرعوا كلوردزامانوا دبرككنسركوغ ابرتوسو

كمن بريموا كسر مثوا ادامى فباد غشكيا فسكن كنبئ

در دونيابنت امثبا كاطبريوكناطورنكغوبى

اغيذ بريمذ ابجنر غشكر كدكج كنز بجنر حسودى

مزفورفرى تنوفركونودا كبز شز بجنر وجلا كنن

اغيذ بزيمذ ابجنر غشكر وندكشرى دومرغوبيى

كلم دبرى سكورسنااملى شناذكرى سنالصلانتنس

شرتبشذ دونيا بتسدوبابا سوخنفلنسرناغفبادس

كبزكلاد فنى زماانى كزكزنكندكوتعبادى

كرنورد

B.

كُرِبُوزِدُو نِبَاتَا طُوبُو الِكُوهِ يَبِطُوَ ذَاشِ شِفَارِ بَنُو الا

تَنَادَ شَرِ طَنَتَ نَفَارِبُوَاهِ ارِسُرِ تَفُو تَكَرِ رِكِ رِسَبَا وَرِي الا

اِرِكَاغَ كُنْبِرَاتَتَ تَلَافِكَدِ غَبَسَ دَبَيِمِ زَاتَ تَغَزَ بَاتِنُو الا

كِبَيْتِ تَبَارِ كِيتِ اَبِرِ تُوتُسَرِ دُومِرِ اَبِنِدِ ذَاشِغِنِ فَرِسَنُو الا

95. دُومِرِ دِزِ اَهِنِي تَدُوكُرِ لِيُورَا اكِسُو وَرِنِفَدُ وِيكِشَا مُوبُو الا

دُومِرِ دِزِ اَهِنِي تَدُوكُرِ لِيُورَا كَلِي كُرِبُوزِوَا نَا اَمُسَا اَبُو الا

اللّٰه عَبِرِ عَجَتِمِ نَكِرِ رُوفُو لَهُ كَدِ شَكِيمِ وَنِرِ كُونِكِي الا

مَعِزَامِ كُونِكِي نَدَاَ مِتَشِنَا دِرِغَا وَرِنِفَدُ وَدِنِبُو بُوَاهِ

كُوبِرِ عُوَاكِبِرِ وَرِبِتِينِي اكُبِرِ يِفِرِتِكِي دِرِ دُنِيَا اُسِرِل

100. اِرِكَاغَ زَاهِنِي يَا اَعَرِ بَاتِي لَا اكَدِ كِرِكِتِي بِعَبَا دِكَاهِ

كِيدِرِ عَبُودِ كُنِدِ كُغَانِفَانِ، دِرِ دُونِيَا تَجَتِ تَلَذَ الاتِنِي

اِرِكَاغَ تَامَتُرَ دِزِ زِبَا تَا بَرِ بِكِ دِرِ كِبِيتِ كُرِ اِيَا اَبُو الا

اِرِكَاغِ صَافِيَا رَا تَلِاخَطِي اِجِرِ حِزِ تَفَصِ كَتَفَتَ بِلَادُوَاهِ

104. نِبِدِرِ اِتَلِ غِتِمَكِ دِنِغِيَا اِحِلِنِدِ وِنِيَا دِرِ كِرِ بِيُورِي الا

دنار طو قوا غونز شيطان سلفا غوالرف موا فكاوا
ما دو يو دونيا حلى سلامتنا في بنع تبتاب غمدكننا
فربيا ابوك باند ما غشك قدكر كنز لكب شا شا شا
دنيا دنار بد مغا غاني كر ميشغشغوا دشر تذنبا
تدر ظلام مو ركيته نتن اغا غ طوقوا غونا النوشا
دنار طوقوا ماتا لجاكر ودند سنكسانا غبر غوشي
شي مي اكر نغمر دنينا و بد وكياد شواد سر ونتنا
كبي ابند برشر ذقا تت كود اشنا دكيا ونجا راوا
يار وا اعنا غيا مكبيل ورا بر سكا كند فرزا اموا
كتبنلا ورنك كشر شربا برند ونيا مر فار لوا
كبر بدا اكبر سركا طوقو اكر متن غبر با طوقوبا
داكر فمر نيا ناكار اشا دا بجمر بسني متن غميابا
دتنفيك يا نك كرلورا يار وشكر متن طوقو نانس
سداد متو اسكر كر ابوا نا غبار سني منم بمنن
كمناكر دونيا دبورنغوري نكر قو اسداد بعينك
اناد طو

B

120 انّ دطر ينتنزي قاسابالا مككخمز طنويه كو غوبر لا لا

بونده تنفو انزا بيبش ورنزن ندو نيبا تيسرنتا ونيبر لا لا

كو ننك دو نيبا بعدو ديبزو باكو تنس بيه كاكاسسن لا لى

نجا برن دو نيبا باانجاني لو سبيما اكمز مسو بيدمنا بن لا لى

دوفر ابند باشرمانتنكا لا كدكد وا بر دككا دامرلا لا

125 كبز تد وكبا الجزدا ادا دى لا لكر فوفزي كشزي غدنفو بز لا لى

نجبز ند و نيبا الاله تتا نزا لكووبه تات شي ربش غوبى لا

بشي ونده بكي ندو نيبا دوزاري لو نمنيه شنكر بشنى شفر اجيبا لا لا

بشي ونده كغ باشر عبادا ابالو كمبرشر دو نيبا نسرنتا روذي لا لا

بإذن مز دو نيبا باانجاني لو شيها كمر مسو بيد منا با لا

130 بارو انا كرتك غدا انجاني لو كادا فلير شرو بكما مسبا لا

بيد وانا غمنك دلاه كولا انزبه جنفيه بكسا مويا لا

بشي ونده بيه نزنشيطاني لو يشنجه نملفذ بيه نمز تور وا لا

بونده كغ نازز ربنا لا لا كد كبيشن نجوزمز شيطو ننى

134 الهاجر هجيتن الهاجر لو كد كسو ابيني الجمو جبنى لى

B.

نِيبَانِشِ بِيبِنِي الْبُوتِيبَا اِرِتَارِ كُوبِتِ حَلِيبَا بَامَا

بِنْدَ اَفَلِ فَلِي بَا الحِ بِنِ بِنْدَ اَبِرِ دِبَاشِ دَاَبِقَانِي مَامَا

دِرِسَا نُوَا بِيبِ دَوَا كِبِيبَا الْمَاجِرِ شِكَبِدِ دَنْغِيبِي مَامَا

اَلْمَاجِرِ شِبِدِ وَكَا يَا بَا اَمُونْدَ كَاتَنَا مِسِرِ الحِ بِينِي مَامَا

كُطُرُفُ وَالْفِيَا مَلِوَا نَارِ كُووِ بَاسِكَا سِبِينِي تَارِي مَامَا

مُودِ رِفَا فِدِ حِمُ بِم بُوبَا دُ وِمِ مِسَامُ تُجَارِ نَفُو بِرِ مَا

دِرِ دُنِيَا دِزَارِ تَفَرِ فَارِي وَكَدِ كَبِيبِ كُهَرِ بِنِ عُبُو بِرِ مَامَا

تَنَارِكِ وَوَاغِيبِنِي كَكَبَا دِمِ مِنِ اَفِكَارِ وَ مَامَا

كِبِدِ زِ اَطِبِرِ تِرِ بَعْفُوا مَابِرِ كُوَوَاشِغِ نِكِبِنِي بِارِ نُفُو مَامَا

تَكْنِ تَلَبَادِ تِرِ سِكِلِكِ دُومِ تِمْبِرِكِ عَمَا الحِ بِرِ مَا

تَنَاشِفَا اَدِ بَدِ رِضَا نُوا دِدُو كِبِكِ كُودِ سِرِ وُنِ مَامَا

كَدِ كَسُوَا بِخِتِ بِرِ كُوَانَا مُخَرِ شِبِنِكِ فِيكِ كَكُورِ تَنَا مَامَا

تَنَادِ زِرِدِ دِرِ تِيرِ نِيَا نَدِ وَكَكَادِ بِنْدِ تَفُو بِشِمَا مَامَا

اِنَا خَنَفِي بِرِ وُدِ سِبَا بِشِغِ رِ بِكِبَا اِرِ فَادِ كُ بَا مَامَا

اِنَا مْنِي كُورَا غَا اَنَا دِرِ اَنَا فَا تَكِلِ تِنْجِيمِ مَامَا

اَنَا غِنِي رِوَا	تَسِرِي

B.

اِنَا غِى زَوَا يَا غُفَبَا   بِنِيرُ فُنْدَ مَا ارِ فَادَ اَبَا
شِنِى وَنَدِ كِيُنْدُ وُنِيَا دُوزَارِى   شِنِى غِنِى بِشِى شِغِ زَامِبَا
دُبَا اَسِرِى سِرِ كِيُدِرِى دُوبَا   اِرِ بِارَاشِنِى بَلَكِى بَصِيرَبَا
كُوبِرِ غُوَا كِجِيرِ كُسُوزَارَا   اِنَادَا بِجَمَا مِنَ اَنْبَانِى
دُوْمِرِ بَوُزِدِمِ بِفَضُولَوَا   كَدِ كِجِبِشِ بَاشِزِدَا اَبِقَانِى
كِيُدِرِى اَنَمِ شِنِى غُمِرِ مَا الْمِى   كِجِيلِكُو لَا خَرِلِكُو دَا اَبِقَانِى
كِبِرِ نَدِ وَكِبَا وَقِيلِى كِبِنِى   بِدِرِ نِسَامِ كُوبِا نِسَاقُوبَا
طُورُ وَرِنْدِ بُو نِمْرِ لُوزَا   نِمِرِ نِشِنِ كُوَدِ عَبَادَاشِرِ
كُزَا اُرِ نِغِرِ زِرِ هَرَا اِبِرُوا   نِرَوَا فِنَدِ نِمِيدِ مُنِمِ كُوبِنِرِ
اِرِ نَا بِفُوبِنِغِ سِرُونَا بَرَ   كِنِ مَا الْهِى دَشِدِ عَبَادَاتِى
بِرِ شَفِ جَاهِلِى مِنْمِ وُوَفِ   نَكِرِ ذُرِشِ بَا كُودَا اِنُوسِوُ
نِجِرِ بِنِ كِوُا كِبِرِ اِنَا مُورُو   كَدِ نَدِ وَغِرِ بِرِ شِرِ بَابِرِ
غُورِ غِمِ بِرَا اِنْتُوفِ جِبِنِ   اِنْجِى مِحِ بِرَاهِى زِ بِيَا زَانَا
قْنَادُ فِلْفِلِى هُزِنَا بُوبِى   اللهُ نِشِكِمِ مَكَ مُبُودُ لِشَا

B.

مُوكِيتُو بِن فَلِيسِ رُوطِي هَشَارِ رِوَاهِمُ مَتِرِمُ كُورِ بَارِي

يَارَبَّنَا غَمِرِ بِكِ نِكُرِ رُوقُوا آلِلْمُشْكِيمُ مَكَ مَنَا فَفِنَا

فَهْجَنَا غَمِرِ بِكِ نِكُرِ رُوقُوا كِبُهِرِ جِنِكِرِ اِمُهِ نَارِلِ

يِرِ مِيهِ مَ حَسَكُو تُتَتَ تَدِرِ أَهِبِ مَرِكُو سُورَ بِرِ

فِبَادِ قَبِرِ ضَنِمِ مَرِزَ اِنْجِي زُوَاهِدِ بِرِ رَاهِ زِبَارِزِنِي

تَنِعِرِ نَفْهِمِ تَنَاجِبِكَ الفَشِّ نَفْهِمِ اِنْبِرِ اِبِرِ فَفِنَا

غَمَا فِبِرِ نِسِ غَمَا نُغِبِرِ عِنْدُو دَا آسْمَهَا غَمَا نُغِبِرِ بُهِمِ

اِزِرِ زِقِيرِ عِنَا زِحَسَكِنَا تِخِ دِبِرِ سِيرِ زِغِمِ فُوبِيِ

اِنِ غِبِيسُوا اِتَادَ دَفَرَاوَا اَرِ الدِّعْلَا نَاشُكُرِ اِكِدِ مِي

طِبِرِ مُمِرِ مِجِي دَامِنِيِشِ نِشِبَارِ اِنْبِشِمِ آبِرِ فَفِنَا

نِشِبَارِ اِلَا دِ مِجِبِنِي دِ نَا اِكِبِرِ هَلِ بِزُوا اِيِخِدُو

وهذا الكتاب شاعر العجمي

ب

يا ربي دنيا ولعيع نا بسر ، دمركطرشي غنة نياء و نيايا

د نبي مختار سيكي ماسوغة تشا ، بلتشا غنز غو مكا فو د و نيا ،

اتكام ملقينا برين جيا هيل ، يا ربي طرشي كع تكتمر د و نيا ،

ني برسينبا ي نكنبا ارساقسا ، كجو و يانكي باسني ياسر كيا ،

د نجا هيلي د با فيني و و فيني ، يا طوطي كينسر بينسنيا غنو و نيا ،

د نجا هيلي غنا و فيني تشيمو تو ، و ينسا بنة اني د مرسانة و نيا ،

كر انكشيمسا تشيكنيبع اسني ، اشطي د د مرطو قيا فرشي يا كيا ،

يا طوفي كينسا د نويا نبع سني ، يا روشكر د مرغنبع غنة و نيا ،

يني باشير غرز رغا الجنتسا ، يا ميع كفنا نيا غبنة ا د و نيا ،

بيسلا كينيا منيو قيا غلا خر ، يا بركي كفنا انتي غجنكر ميتيا ،

بيسر غد انشر بنايد ابسا ، يا كرتي كا بيتي غجعر لر د و نيا ،

بيسنا طفر اكوينيا تر انكي تشا ، بينة فني يا يا ترابغ ترد و نيا ،

كيشركة و و كيمكر تو سيتا ، كيبة مركا يا د امتايشي د و نيا ،

بيسر د ربنة عكربي و تسا ، يني تمهسر د و ما تشا د و نيا

ارو ا د ما تا د و ما يطي تشا ، كينور و او غا فقر و سو د و نيا ،

c.

واو كيشي وايليند زو ودونيا، ميهنقلي كرغار طلو جل دونيا،
ميهنكلي شيرابو كر صالح، شيفر غوه منا اتاكي تاكر دونيا،
كرتا غمي كتلو طير اتاها كري، اكثر تهو يافر كيا ميكر ونيا،
ارتا تهو تاكو قطر نرد كا، كغطو بوطي سيجو رج دونيا،
اركا غطو جتركيني متاكو نتا، اتيطي دكى كريا كيكي مرغر ونيا،
ارتا غمو قد كيرد دتفو ركوا، قل تار كاده يا ربو جاه دلا اجيا،
ارتا يا علقتو ليري د كيقا باتجلكا شبا، كورو كسو نتا اشي تكي كر دونيا،
ارتا يا علقو ليري د كراتو لوبي، كرسيرتا بود يو كو وا دونيا،
ار دو كيا تبا كا امشي و تكي، ار لا جيا باكا طرزهم جليبيتا دونيا،
اركو جيا تباكا امشي و تكي، كسيني جكو تاده اجلي دونيا،
اركو تسر و تا اغر يكطرتتا، راتر عقر كوه دونيا يا لا جيا،
كماياب مرتار شفو دونيا، كماياب مرتار بتاده غدو نيا،
دويا غجار مردي جرند كقيقيا، كوكا شكيمتا رشقو دونيا،
ونيا غغاور مرتيا لا فتر، كوكا مكيمتا دتر بيتاده دونيا،
ارده منا جي بيني تكا سنغا جر، بركا مكي ملا دتر بيتاده دونيا،
انده وكي يا كو كي تكي غرما القيم، دنجا هلي باو تني انده دونيا،
دو تكو ده اميكر تني نقا الميم، كر جي تكر غمه اجا هلي انده دونيا،
ده يا جيا يا تكي قد اده ما اليم، دنجا هلي سيكو تريج سر غمو نيا،
كوكسو شيتي ما يا كو كيتا، اشيره كو ميا ترغم اكر دونيا،
سيكو ابتني تيا نشا نسا كرجيا، سيكو تقا اكيبه اغم اكر دونيا،

عفير ولول

f

عقبر فلول

عقبر فلول كذ نغذ نقبير نسا، كو وكبير نسر باشطير اكنجيا

كور كيا صلاة كذ نذ يار ما المعري، ركرا از [illegible] زكري كي ركر كو نغم ونيا

شوني تغوبير مو ومني نشير نقوا، د نبيا امطيو غكوا د ونيا

كو وكبر شاو د عور سنغموا، يلن وقبيسر د وككا نر د ونيا

يار بمر روكي كا طير الاخر، كطر يقا د نبا ونكع نبا د ونيا

كطر يا ونر تر بر نبر ساوكا، اكطر د د نغيمو غذ نجا د ونيا

اكطر د الفم بنى محمد، ار سنبر سبر ولع بيوا العو ونيا

واكاغ د نبا وخليل قبيا، القاضي نكو شيغني قسنوسيا

د نغر عو نسبا د وسنا الاهو، د نكر عبا نسا بيصنا وكر جيا

شي د نغر جيا بن عو نسر زينب، شوين عبا نسر سيد المختار كر جيا

الله نسركي د نبيا سو غاقبر، د ومر قبشيفو سنوسر شينو بويا

يلر بسند سنوسر نبير د ونيا، د نالاخر ابشيسر غير نيد وغر بيا

نا شر يا كا بنا غشيفو سنوسر قنا د ونيا، نيا د وكي كو وشيع بلر نيا

الحمد لله قنا د غو د يا، غير جل سركي و د بيوا د ونيا

ثم صلاة على نبي المصطفى، غير د نر جيع بجة و د يكي هد ونيا

شي غير كبا كو مر غذ اكر د ونيا، بر و نيو يا با بلي شد يو د ونيا

ار يعي د وطو سنر د مهقسر د ونيا، د ومر بكدا انا بكلا با غع ونيا

يع و تلو نث با يبي مسا د ونيا، د نر جمع قسر ايكلو را قبيا

كدو وب سر و د بيوا الا ونيا، يا طير با شي غني غذ ابا كر جيا

نقت بقع الله واكا انا [illegible] نكا، غير قبل سركي و د بيو د ونيا

D.

بسم الله الرحمن الرحيم صلى الله على سيدنا محمد وآله وصحبه وسلم

هذا كتاب الراعي ...

[illegible]

D.

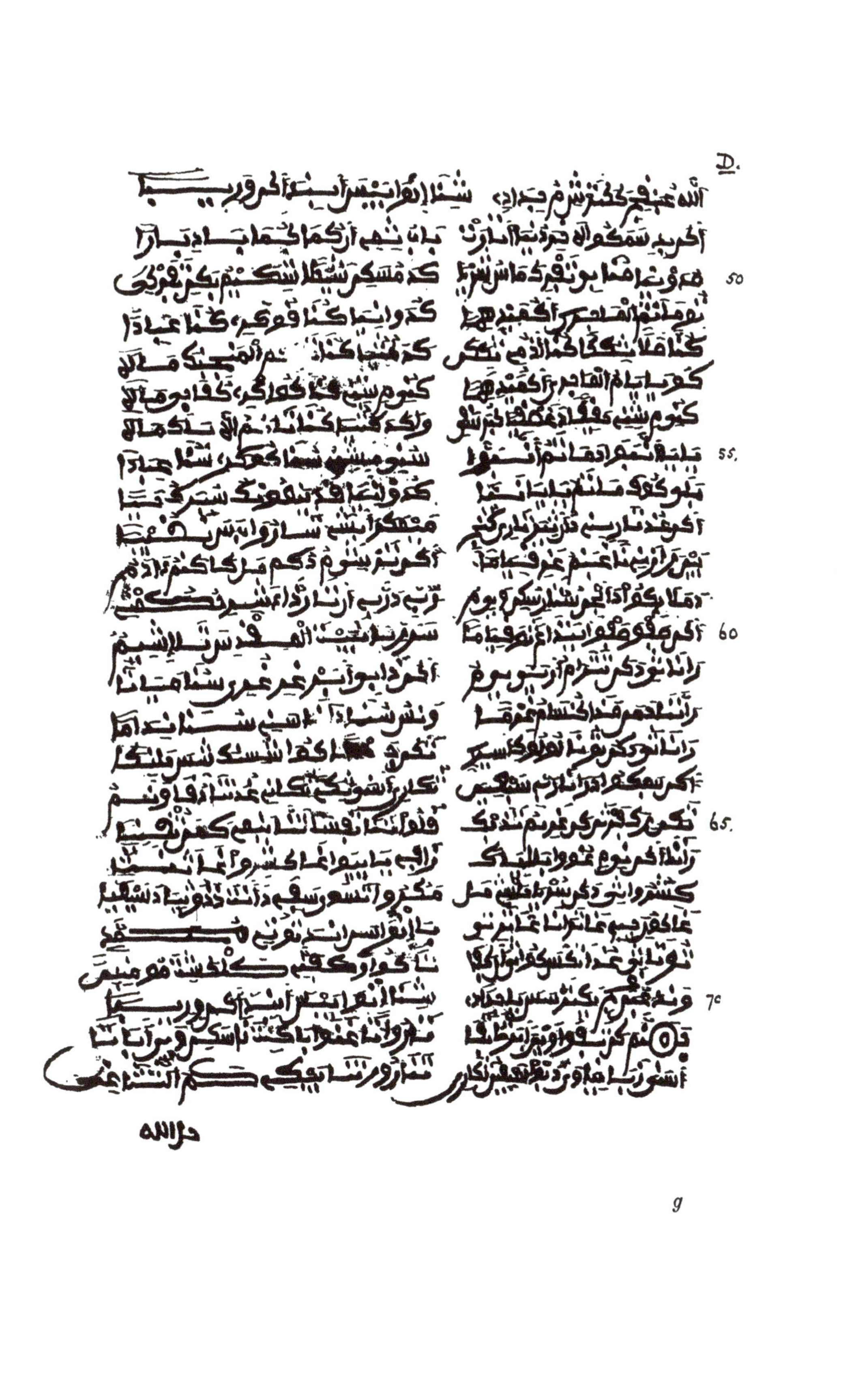

D.

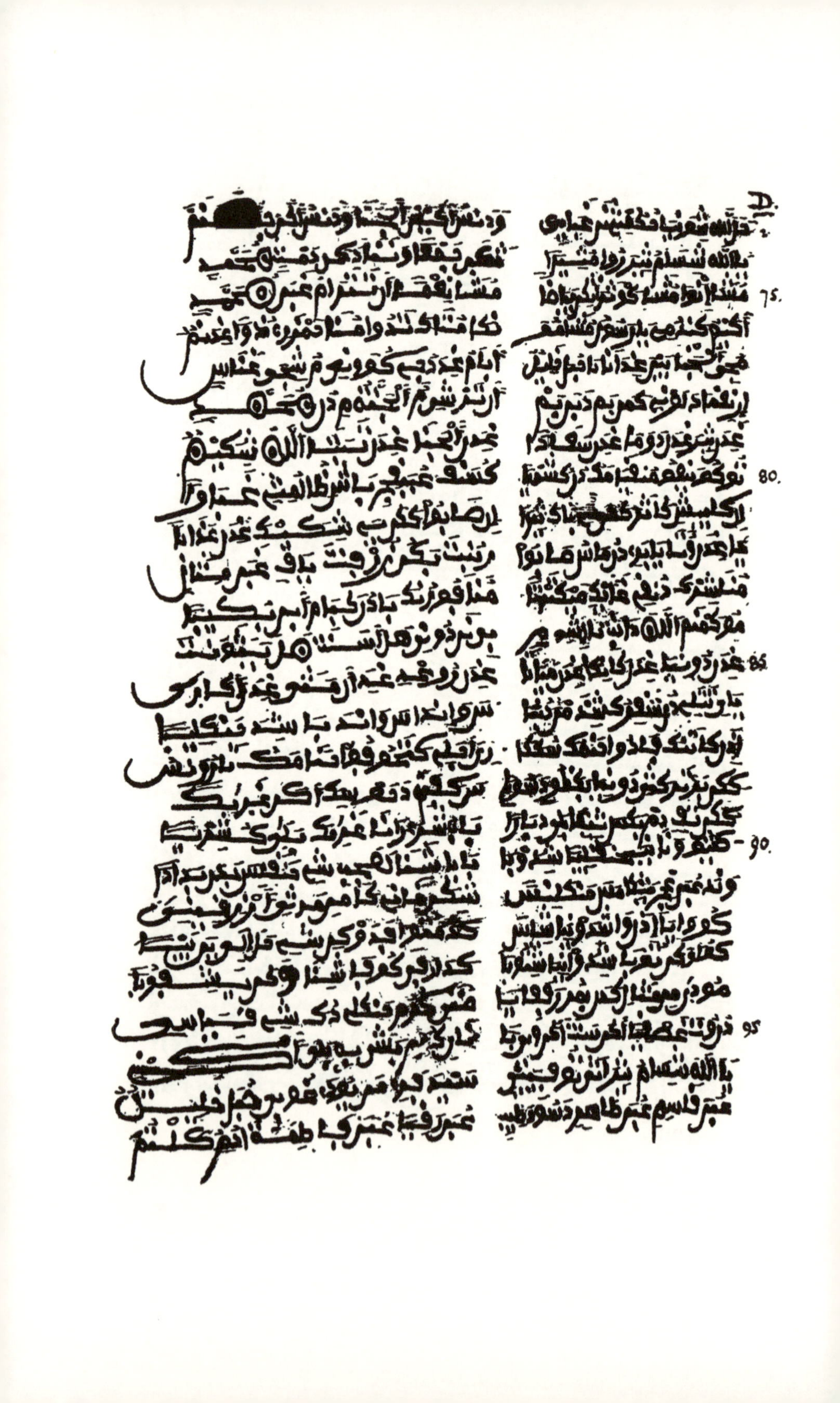

D.

D.

قلوا الله الله شادا دسو كيشرا دا منى ديرا فشيدنا محمد

ئبرا نعام الله دبر يشرهم امثنى لفشت غرمجبو دو اللو محمد

100. اقرا الحمد لله منوم بيو الله مفا اشكرا مفا غودبا دوا غلا الله

اقرا الحمد الله منوم بيوهي مفا اشكر مفا غودبيا دو الحمد

الحمد لله رب العالمين

الصلاة والسلام

بسم الله الرحمن الرحيم   صلى الله على من لا نبي بعده

مغو نره بر نغ سركر سووت   ديا ايكو محمد درامينا

منذ يالطاه بسلا جيبي   د له ماتر قصد ياي كووا

كسوزر اجما الفاد زاوا   علنم دعنك ذانه اسن منوبا

ديبنشي منيبللش بالشطير   منوبا مبز بنللش كومطيرا

كبرسر قيذ اليبرنا اسنا   ابرغاد ينق بايي عنك كوالسي

اذ رمنذ وجهاد مرش السنا   اغرغمد وكينسر اكوماتا

اذ ار كوماتا ازربانا   زبوند وكي دميذ وي اجلسي

وتدالكازند باذواد ويعامر   منوبا دشر غلوزكة مكونا

د الفضر دما السرذ واشربه   كنوبا اكيوبير سرذ شيابا

اذ ركيرذ وبنم كبنذ بتى   دشر موجه كذ وب تلزد ثرني

اذ رعنكي فيكم نزد ومقربا   مطرشز غمود منيبكود كووا

اذ رانجو نوبشي جهاد   مذو مودد وكيا منتي دماتا

ذا مذ كالسر فيمد ومرضور   اكيفخذر كياسر كسام لاادا

دَمَاسُ نْبِرَ آمَارُ سُوكُنُوبْ   وَظَا لَمِيُرْ لَسَرُوْنَا أَنْرَنَا آسْنَا

كُبْرُ مُدْرَادَ ظَا لَمِيُرْ مُسْلِمِي   كَدَا آمُولُوكُبْرُبَا وُدَكَرُمَا

دَمَاسُ رُوْ وَامُسْلَا بَادُرْسِدَمْرُ   سُنَادُو بُرْ قِرَامُ لَسَرْكَ تُوبَا

دَمَاسُرْ دَمَاغَنْ بُومِرْ مُسْلِمِي   كُنُوبَا كُبْرْ قِبْسَادِ كَدْ كُكُونْسَا

دَمَاسُرْ دُوَا غَكُو فُو مِرْ بَرَانِي   سُنَارْ تِرْكَلَنْبُرْدُوَا غَمَانْسَا

كُنُوبَا كُبْرَا بِرْ نُرْمُنْتِ بَنِي   إِدَرْ كُوكُرْكَ تُوبْ دُوكَ كُونْسَا

(21) دَمَا سُو بِدْرُو بِشِي وَ إِدَرْ آسَنَارْ   آنَا عِبُورْ نَدْ كُرْ كُرْكَ تُوبَا

دُوَنْدَ قَابَاكَ بِرْ بُورْنُه بَادَمْ   سُنَارْ غَدَا دَسُودُو نُرْ بِجِيمَا

كُنُوبْ كُبْرْ كِبِي كُرْدِي سِي   كُبْرُمْرُ جَلْسَدُورْدَ دُكُرْ بِيَا

(22) دُوغَرْمُرْكُمْرُ دُوْنَبْ دُسِرْ آمَارْ   كَدَمْ شِكْ الْكُوزْ آكُبْرْ نَكْرُ بَا

مُسْلِمِي وَنْدَبَا لَسُودُرْ لَه وَانْزُ   سُنَارْ غَدَا دَ آحْمَدُ دَوَا هِمِيْنَا

كُسُورْرَا كُنْ مَغَنْ مُسْلِمِي   آبِرْدَ آكُبِي قِدَا أَمُرْ غُشْكِيَانْسَا

(24) إِدَرْ دَرْكُرْكَ تُوبَا آبِيدِ بَسُو   إِدَرْبَا سَانْرُ بَابْ دَمَا غَكُووَا

إِدَرْ لَسَرْكُرْ مُسْلِمِي دَابِرْ مَدَّ   آكِيمِرْ آدَغُمْ آمُسْنُرْ بَكَابَا

جَابِيمِرْ شِ

بايمن بيزم شي ازاكيمم   مطر ككذو شين مكو تنوبا

مزويا بر غذ نم شبامايك   منانز شكر جمد انغاج زاوا

دصالحين دموم نكبنانز   مزويكا بر غذ نم شكابم تابراي

منابجني دكابرزكك مز   اكبر مزوتاو ننا انا شيد كبابا

مزويكا بر غذ سركر سروت   اذ منانز مبغذر دانسنا

دمانرمود بابرم دبيزو   ددو كوكر ملسلم ذامناباي

مكدبرمو غراغرمود طوبي   وبنركك ذلم دكك ذامسناباي

مكو انجي باب كشر واباب بنو   شكر داد منامزنا دجونا

بر الله دابركو ولسيبي   بكابم غرد عندك رب دغفووا

اذ منبنزركابمنك تريش   تتنب مكل بيوا حربكورا

اذ منانزد بزنر بكورا   مذوبزنر تلات نرمكانا

اذ منانزد بزنر تلات   نجاد مكل بيا وانرمكانا

اذ منانزد نرم بينمم   تدر عيشي د بر غذ دامكانا

44 إذر منتا يرد نر متني حم مدومو كتر كنش امسد كابا

هر الحنو د بنوث مبر ير نون مد ومو كرز قبا امسد كابا

إذر منتا يرد نر متني حم مد ومو مد رغنا غلبر وكار

إذر منتا يرد نر متر يحم مبيلا امبكبس حم اد ما وا

إذر منتا يرد نر اد ماوا مد ومو كلسر بخو امسد كابا

ينكا يم غرند بابرنش غفوا يشكر د اد مساء د لار يباوا

إذر منذو فا صنار مند كبوت مدا غني مد كحت موبشر مدينا

منذ نب الطاها بلا محمد د البر محمد بابا كووا

52 صحبن نو د تابع تبعين منيمر الله عد امسام حبرا

كمل قصيدة السفر
اسم المكاتب رمضان بن
يوسف بحمد الله وحسن
عونه الصلاة والسلام
على رسول الله

E

بسم الله الرحمن الرحيم — صلى الله على من لا نبي بعده
مغودي جز سركي مزايباوا — تكلكل جل امز ابكو دكوا وا
مناكم برصلاة بسا محمد — دعال دصحب دجمع النبا وا
دتابع تابعين داوليا — دامالاكوا مناكم سلعوا
قبيشر كو صلاة دسلعوا — كسوزا ر اجماع العلما زاوا
قيا كن كوا اوانا صاحبينا — كطرتتر اتنفعمر بيار كوا
ابو كينا ككرة كتوركا — ابنة تكي قطامك بابوا وا
كبركم جاسداد مهي دقرنا — فرازادكا كبز داغي فكوا وا
كتوف تميز قرانم دود صابو — كبز فز بيا ككفرتيز زكاد كوا وا
كبركم عن دا رجا تهعولا دسوا — كبز شا شا كبز غو بش عكوا وا
كبز دز كدار كا دكه سانا — كطرتش تعوا دمز ابكوا دكوا
كتوب كبز وبهر منكر ددانب — كتوب كبز هز زو فوا اكوا وا
كتوب دانمقيغ ذكد زوا — كبز زد كد فلا الفسق عكوا
كدز دو قو ككيسور رو والله — دمانشين عن صبا دكوا
دما نشين كبا دكا بيا الجسانا — دماشبين كزيز دبز كزاوا
دما نشين تسعين تقعين ندا ج — قبنشين كوكر بصر دبا تساوا
كتوب كبز ربك كيد دزكا — كسترشتعود هن ابكو دكوا
كدز يكع زكاكو كيتشر جا — وتلاهز كيشر كيدا ب واوا
قطابزوا كا بهن بكنتو ووز — وايل دكوا الزمز تتبيا وا
كبز شرد وكفنه بامز ايوا — ككلا يغز تعوا دمز ابكوا دكوا

ولادس

وَلَاذِ تَفُرَهُوَا مَزَا آتِيتِيمِ دِلِيَرَكُوَا آكِمِ مَرْتَتِبِيَا وَا
نَسِ كِتُوبَ كِبَرْبِدُ قَلَا غَرَ مَقَاكِ بِغَرَ مَنْدَاكِ كُوزَ مَزَايَا وَا
كِدَ رِكَاطَ شَرْكِي مَزَا يَاوَا آيِيكَا آغَرَ مَقَاكِ قَبَابُ وَاوَا
بِقَلَا يُوزَ اكِرَ مَكِمِ تَفِيغَا دِلِيرَكُوَا كِمِ مَرْتَتِبِيَدُ وَا
يِكِبَرْبِدُ غَاكَا يَكَتَ سَرَ آحَمْ جِيبِيَا آتِيتِيمِ دِيَادِي كُوَا
دِلِيرَ مَرَغِ وَاقَادُ وَنِ غَفُرْوَاز دِلِيرَكُوَا آكِمِ مَرْتَتِبِيَا وَا
آبُوكِبِنَا كِسَرِنِ جَاهِلِيْنَا إِنَا يَغْفِرِ رَسُولِ دِيَادِي كُوَا
كِيَجَ بِدُوشِيمِزِكِ دِسَرَ آبَاكِ تَعَلَرَ شِيكِبَاكِ شِيبَادِ رِكُوَا
كِبَرَسُورُ رِفِشِ بِدِرَ اوَآنَا كِنَا سُوَا وَرَاشِرَ كِمِ كَاوِي كُوَا
كِنَا كِمِ كِسَبِرَا وَكَاوِي كُوَا كِنَا دَا اغَرِ مَنَا بَرِكِيشَا وَاوَا
مَنَا بَرِ نَايُبِيكَ جَدُ رِكَيَاسَ سِنَا شِرِ وَارِكِيدَ عَكَاوِي كُوَا
كِنَا كِمِ شِشِيكَا غَرَ مَرِيَهُوكَا كِهَشَرَ دُونِبَا تُكِبَ وَاوَا
قَارَ دَرِ كَاجِ نَاوَبَادِ رِغَوَا نَا كِتُوبَ كِبَرَشِبَا وَاكَاوِي كُوَا
بِكُوَا سَابِكَ يَادَا ابِيكَ دُنِيَا كِقَابِرُ دُرِ تَعَلَرِ هَرَايَا وَا
بِدُ وَمِرِكِمِ كِنَا سَابَرِ تَعَلَرِ بِنَا غَا يَنِكَ سَرْكِي مَرَايَا وَا
كِسَرِ دُرِ كِنَكَنَا جِرِ غِرِ غِرِبِنَا كِطَرَ شِرِ غَفُوَا دَهُمَ آيِكُوَا غَكُوَا
كِسَرِ دُنِيَا مَيُوتَنَا بِرِ آبُوَاكِ كِدُو بَا آلَنْبِيَا وَاهَابُ كُوَا
كِحَوبَا تَرِ غَا لَدَمِ دُكُ بِنَغَطَ كِبِسَرِ تَتِعِ إِنَدِ مَرَ آيِكُوَا دَكُوَا
إِنَا إِدْرِيسَ نُوحِ كِدَا دَهُودَ كِبِسَرِ تَتِعِ إِنِدِ سَرْكِي مَرَايَا وَا
تَاتَا كِتُوبَ كِكَا قَلَاشَرِ كُطَرَشِرِ غَفُوَا آدَمِ يِكُوَا غَكُوَا اوَا
كِتَلِبَا وَجِمِرِكُو كِطَرَ شِفَ لَلَٰهِ نُوتَا غَكُوَا اوَا
دَوْلُوَ يَلِرِ يِدَ لِيَا اشِرِ غَكُوَا اوَا دَوْ لُوِيَلِرِ بِكِنَا آسِيمَرْهُو

اندكم صالح نغفل سودك   كسرته عند سركي مر ايداوا
اندكم شي قبلر الله شي كوا   قبلاته عند مرايكواد كووا
اندا اسمعيل سما ايبر سودك   كسر كوما غذا يتر هرايداوا
انديعقوب حزنجبكس سودك   كسرته انده مرايكواد كووا
اندموسى دهر ورد لوط   كسرته انده سركي مرايداوا
اندعيسى دذ الغرنير سودك   كسرته انده سركي مرايداوا
انداوود قرد انشر سليمن   سرو تادو نيد بسبرم كووا
كسر دك سرنع دك انده اظا   كسر جبه رشي بيذاب كووا
كدو بالغرجبيبر النبا وا   محمد النبي منم دبياي كووا
دالغرمرود نر النبا وا   حمد لله بام كك اوزشكاوا
كسر جبا رشي بيذاب كووا   تعلم جر ميعيكواد كووا
اندكم هلهلة رسبجنه نمر   انده نمرود ميتر كدجراوا
اندهنده ادمر قصر القشير   اندا جالوت ميتر كدجراوا
اندا قنذر اندا عوج غد نيا   سعو عوزميد غمركدجراوا
سهاما رشعا زور غد نيا   دسنك ودا اشايوشر باسر كووا
اندا يغيش مشر دتار ملكي   دنا مسلمتا خير النبا وا
اندا دقيد نسر بوزغد نيا   دسرك ودات يوشر باسر كووا
اندكم شي ابو جهل دقارن   انا سوليه ميتر كدجراوا
ابولهب مسيلم حرابر   شنسترالاخرايو باسر كووا

كسر

كشرذ بيا كذ هكيجو جقاوا   آذا كيرا الأرض امك تبتاوا =

كذ ركا اشوا اكا لكيذ و نيبيرغا   كشر كتر ذرى كعنتاوا ركشوا

كذو بي شرا اكنا ذكمر ميذ   سنا شرا الأخر ايو باسر كووا

كبيو فرنا ذ يقمر نرنذ نيبا   كشر ذربا و بيانك سنبليوا

كشر سام غبير سشر مجمع   ذا ايقار ذ بكا اور شكلا اوا

كشو تكنبيم عيرى دكشر بيا   بيبر تعبيرذ باب ذما غكووا

ذما تعبير ذ با غنزي غنذ نيبا   غذا ابا بشر بتعقبا بشي غكووا

بشر تعبير تشذ بارا اكو موا   كذر كاسا عقبا باو بيو يا اوا

كشر بيا ذاك بررخ ذر غوانا   كذر كاجيك باكم ذاو بيووا

كشر ذو فيترغ ناب بفر كذ ها كونشر   ذاكبر شر قبا ابو اوا

تنا ذكمر غير كو با غربيا   كشرذ نيترغ مذ تنك بذ واوا

قار ذر ذ اغر ببشر ذو نبيرغا   كا اشكر ومر سليرو النبا وا

كذو با شر غنا ذم آو لينشر   قبسر تنكه حر غا خصذ يدو كووا

عمر ازر ذ غ كو انا ذر غوانا   كطر بشر قكر بنشبا تنشكر كنشوا

كطر بشر قرنذ منو انا بشما   ذباك منيري قكا تكه بابو اوا

ابا ببر جرا اوا ك سبجر و بيك   سنا ذر و اغر اك ذكر با ضغ ابا وا

آكا و ما غنيغ اجقا ابا كـ   سبا ك كشا قدم و كتلام عبوا

٤٠

حنا ميفة كنا قدا رادنييشي مشوا كا انا مرنيتكاوا

إذوا يشع بوكيشي ززتيا يشع هسوة انا كا سترة كم تسلهاوا

و دنسر سنا مصلى و نسر كو كا فبكر كاسدا فبدا باو يويا وا

دييلرا ابير دمه تابر ككوكا هوانا نبلغ ايكر هو ايا وا

دييلرا دمه تانسي

هذا انتبر كهنغرا اكتر كذ بنا فيايكر جزيا بذ دمه عكووا

شنه فزميرقبل دزياشرا يكوا فبيترا يكونتر سترك ميرا يده

انا فغر منغ نهك انا مسوا فبيو كتر درككنتا وكبشو

انا فزبير قهانسر يمنك كلم فبيو سو نبرا كيك و دريكبشوا

عشر فزيا شكيمك باشر شنك فبسر منزيا ك ايكو بيو دكوا

اكا فو در همير كم ذ اايشرتيا اذ مكدك انا كم غر عقلوا

و دنسر شند شرد اشر فعر كشبلوا انه ستار رانا شر دركبشوا

اكا ما قازوا اعقاد كضوا او نكبر كا فبشر ذ مر كيشوا

اسلامك ركعفر كم اشغبر افبشك عنوا كرناك واوا

اطيبه صفوا اصلا بنك كيتنوا فبكر بكسر ا يندا كيبه واوا

ادرشر فايرصلا كم سدوكا سكيك شو نكطاك يشكر كشبوا

اكا فو درانا شر كم اجسترا تكا بنر و نسر كوشك اكلداوا 94

دكر و

F.

اكا وو درحكى عشبرا درهسى كجا يكر دكا ادرهيقا كيسوا

اكوب فسدا اناكم للباوا اجا وو بكر فسستا كركشسوا

سونكبر حتونسر كذا افجا بوا ستا كم بغيسو رجو نا غكووا

سوا شبرا شو سبركى نكركبسوا كلوكى دكنكى باب ورى فتووا

ازرب دوكيبركى ادورمزنا فيدا بابرا بدسا ابيتوكووا

بكدر صتادكر بابكدنا كا عزوا بانتا بشكى يشكركبسوا

نكبر دمنكر سبعتوا غبركى كند قبرنكى كيد ربدب كووا

ادنذ هومصر ككم بوابا فينهم الترب تنا يشكى دوكبسوا

ترابر دكا نا الجنا دنعما دخو بنعبرنا بدوكنبه لوا

مكا يكوا اشعام نادكنشر يشكر النور قباب دبولا كنوا

ادركو جاسغ ككيكدغ ذلا نكبرسبكر ورپك يشكر كبتسوا

ستدير كنك قركو بنركبنبا كنا كو كا انا قم عدغدا وا

كلا كر فرقنا سكذ نبد اقا كنا نيبنم انا مر نيمكا وا

كبسوا انا قطبك شنا بغنك كذ منا نرتشرب حركيندا وا

كنا مر دك سو عتيا صنيد امر دسو سويسم دكم نكك بنغلا وا

سنبر قباك عيكر بركتا وا كذ منا نرتشركم باب كووا

كذ منا نرجم زنر فيا ما جنير نرقرك ونيشكتد كووا

ابو سقفوا ابتنا نيزدكا اتانير قبسا عدد قرانا زو ورى كبيا وا

صبوا كو قرد بوفقبيسر كجو دابكر قرنا ستو كمى قرايا وا

F.

قيرانا تدكستوا كير هتا بن ١٠ تتا فونا قكي تورانو قبتوا

بحاشر زند قبز نر سوك كميا سند دوبي مغنيا نا خبولي

هنا بحفرد قد سفو ككميا مستدزو اشفوا دجقو اكي بحرو

آنا كو كا فينزوا كيت جنوا آنا اسك باب دك موعدا غداوا

مل بكرو تاشر كبرو وبيرد ك دابكر قبر سرك هر ايا وا

آنا كو كا قبكو وانا تكينقر قبا مو تبحكا مك باب كووا

إد قبسير فيد قايا طوتيا اذو د غمر تليبرد آتنبا وا

بد و مرا ام شذ و سر غمبر سرك قبجز قلا زهو ايكو ه كووا

شنهر يا آدم كبنز ابد هو كيبفو اغا غجنم ايد وا

بشنبز بقو بدرا يكو اغكتبنا قبسر كو نوح كوق نشند ايداوا

آذو بي غنوح بلنهز هتابنر كذو اغخليل آسير مرابد وا

آخذ و غخليل ابرهيم نبيكوا نشمسر بقو تبارا يكر سرد كووا

كذ وك غهو سر بيا كوبيرا وانا نشذ و بنز غمبر امرا بكو د كووا

إذ رانذ و اغمر بيشر بيشر ككوما غعيسى نبجر غسرك مر ايلوا

إذ رانه و اغعيسى بيشر ككوما غلا قصدا السينم دبادي كووا

ذما نبيني شفيع الكلق نبير آمير الله آحمد يابادي كووا

آخذ و قعير ابنشر هسر يا محقو بدو و بشنم كبنز كدو كووا

نشند بنر اقتنى بد كبر سيز كه هو غذك دو كيبنز مرابدوا

نشجاد نشنا بنجود عتد ذا اقتنى نشما بنر اقتنى بد امر ايد وا

اشر مسر

F.

اسنِ متونيا نسِ كننك قبيا محمد   قتاب سمبود يوكو كداي كووا

قبيرِ ككسوا املك قبيا محمد   قمر دِ ابك كيبنر كداي كووا

ننهر ينتوا نبكسوا ابا الهي   جبار جلا آمر جيكوا اذ كووا

انبر انبا ك آيكمسر دو قساي   ذ ابكر جار سرك مرايد قوا

بقدر انا قبا تونا الكرد ك   جسغم تا قبا توا ايا ب وا وا

ذ ما ع وبا زبك بنر تيغا   قبا ايا نرد ليليبنر غكووا

زفا ار كو جساب تو زابكا   او نتر اكر ج ميزان غكووا

آجنعوا كو تكرد رايكم   مسلم تلداام سكجو رغا وا

كما بغم دقا سغي ككوكا   تكرد وتا سر خور سعكبر رقا وا

عدو وركر انبورا انبورا   عذابا تا ابشس و قباب وا وا

بلا ركك كو صراطي نير جيما   آنا سر آخود ايكو مرايلوا

دكبيع كود سمطي دك سوكا   قرمتا تنسر وغاشر بابيو وا وا

دبوكوحر الف بشمكر اك ف   حوا نسر حر سو ونسر باب وا وا

صراطي مني تو ذو نير بكينبر   قسود ك تنقيبا بنبم نكووا

غنو ذ نير بعوكوا كلاج توكيز   آبكر كم تنبيرك قباب وا وا

نير لفوا قصلا كلاج نفكك   نغبا بكلاج آذمي بابي وا وا

غنو ذ بنبير كلاج زكا   آبكر كم تنبير ك قباب وا وا

نيند قبرا يلا بير كلاج وا وا   آبكر كم تنبير ك قباب وا وا

امر دبو تا كم ذهني دمنكر   آبكر كم تنبيرا نبكر غكووا

F.

يكون كاذو سودى كوزر فيامنا غيرا ليمنا شرىك كىتبنا وا
يكون بكنوا دمتو بقو لسر كفا كسر كرى نروتا ككك غنقر اوا
صر ايلي وانسر كرشو بجم واشكا ودنسر يو كفيا كم بابو اوا
ودنسر كم غدو وسر تشر تشر ودنسر دجو جكي شك فيشترو اوا
جهنم داشر تشفا كم اكورا بسودك ملا سيم تفا غكوا
جماعتر موهمر سكعشتر لوا جماعتر جدا سيغو با فيشتر لوا
جماع يوسر تو سيو الذيحر غسوره زهمر دليلشي غكووا
ابشر بحد مشو امايكا بشر اسوكد شبهار قمر شنغ ياب مسوا غكووا
ابشر بحد شوا كجا دوتا كم وما نشر كم باب هشوا دو غكووا
جما يوسر شارا دكلوا تا ابشك دليركوا اكر قمر تمبيا وا
شنا كم بيع يا سوسير ندا اما مشا بشر ليتمنا يو بابشر كووا
ويوم يقوم الطامة تا ابشك دليركوا اكر قمر تمبيا وا
اكبشر غلظم حمر سغرا دخطما تششفا حر ستهير ريد واوا
اكبشر رحيم هلوو قبو غجلو سلا بشكى غدا ابجار سك غسفر اوا
بشر دغ هلوو شتر اكر ابامر اكبشر غمو غمرزكم تبنا وا
اكر كم هلاسر غرمركم غمرنسر غبو لسر ناج شتر سك تبنا وا
قمسرز دا اكشر غمو نهو بمز غبيهر ناج شلر سك تبنا وا
اكر كم قسر قمرزكا غرنسر غسكو ناج شلر كم تبنا وا
ا نفمسر كلسكر كرا ابدا غدا ابا ابشم قسر بدسرى كمبيهكا وا

جماعمر

E

كَتَايِتُوا أتُبِيرِكِيزُوا وَ لَ ‏ وَيْتَا أمْرِكُوَ دِ لِيبِ بَابُ وَاوَا كَ

وَاَيْتَا كُمْ كِدَ الاَيْكِيسِبِرْ ‏ وَيْتَا بِيرِ نُرْ دِ لِيپِيشِرْ أَنْكُوَوَا

اَكَرِكُمْ عَلَاشِرْ فِرْبَادُوَ غِرِشِرْ ‏ وَمِنِيسِ نَاجِ جَارِ سِكَ تَبْتَلُوَا

اَكَرِكُمْ مَلَاشِرْ فِرْ لَحُوَ اغِرِنِشِرْ ‏ غِرْهُمُهُ اِنْدَ سَنِيشِ مْمْ قَبِسَلُوَا

شُكَرِ مْرِ فِيشِ شِيبِكِرْ دِكِ غِبُوبِ ‏ شِيبِيكِرْ دِكِ جُوَوِ بِرِ كِدِ جِرَاوَا 175

شِدُوَ رِكَرِ رِهِمَالِكِ بِيَا بِتِنِشِرْ ‏ جَعِمْ وَتَنَادِ دَرْ هُمُهُ بَابُ وَاوَا

شِيجِرِ بِيَا قَالِكِ شِرْ رُوُوَ مِتُوَا ‏ سُمْسَامِ وَتَنَاوُ تِرِغِمْ سُسَامِ عِغُوَا

جِتَابِيُوسِدْ رِجِتَادُوَ اَتَا اِشِكَ ‏ دِلِيپِرْ كُوَا اَكُمْ مُمْ تَنِتِيبِيَا وَا

وِتَابِيرْ مَكِنِيرْ دِ كِينِيشِيرْ ‏ دِ لِيپِرْ نُرْوُ تَنَاكِمِسِكِ سَكِ تَبْتَلُوَا

جَمْسِرْ زِنَا اَكِبِشِرْ غِرْ رِمُغِنِيَا ‏ غِبِبُ مْرِرُوُ تَنَا سُسِكِ تَبْتَلُوَا 180

اَكِيشِرْ بِيَا قَلِيمْ سُعُتُوا أَعْذَ أبَدَ ‏ جِعِمْ هِمِبْهِ بَابُ شِدْرُ سِكِ تَبْتَلُوَا

اَكِيبِرْ غَوِمِيرْ وُنَارَا رَرُوُ تَنَاجِرِ ‏ غُوَادِ الْفِتْرِ شَارُ سِكِ تَبْتَلُوَا

سُسِعَ الاَيْكِبِيرِ رَهِقُ رُسْعِبَادَرَ ‏ كُنَاهُوَمُمْ سَجِرَ اِ بِتَا وَا

دِكَرِ نَكِلَانِكِرُوُتِ مَلَاشِرْ قِعِبِشِي ‏ سُنَا قِعِبِشِي سُنَا بِيَاقِيدِ طَاوَا

وَتَاكُوغَاتِ تَبْرِ فِيشِ دُوُ قُوتَا ‏ تِنَاكَرِ بِيُرِ غِبُوبِرِ كِدِ جِرَا وَا 185

اَتَنَا اَمُرْ شَاسِرِ نُوَتَنَادِ طَلُوَا ‏ وُتَنَا تَنَا كِيُوُ بِيسِرْدِ طَاوُ تِدَوَا

شُنَا طِرْكَرْ جِجَاعِ الْكَاعِرَاوَا ‏ شُنَا كُوكَا اَنَا اَمُرْ عَلَا عَذَا مِرَا

مَلَا يَكُوَا اَسْطِيدِ دُعَا دِغِنِشَا ‏ شُغِمْرُوُ تَاسْنَا كِمْ عَلَا وُتِدَوَا

اَكِيبِرِ شَعِوُ وِمِيَا مُرْدُرْ شِتَاوَا ‏ زُوَرْ ذَا اِبِ جِتِبِي تَنَا دِيُوَوَا 189

1

[illegible] 190
[illegible]
[illegible]
[illegible]
[illegible]
[illegible] 195
[illegible]
[illegible]
[illegible]
[illegible]
[illegible] 200
[illegible]
[illegible]
[illegible]
[illegible]
[illegible] 205
[illegible]
[illegible]
[illegible] 208

E

قبل يوكته نفعد كيكا دليلى كوا اكر مرتبجد وا
شدو ركرى قبهالك سرقتوبا اكيم غدو ينيد ضب قيبا يد وا
تبشعر كمر كدوم شكر غدا با قدا مر كوكنيم ابكر ا تبدوا
قيكبشر واغنوش الا افرنر دبا كومو قدو ركيكا بحر اوا
قبكبشر بابا تابشر باغدا با ككوكد كنك يا الكا بحوا وا
فصل
جماع الهو منرد كر مرا طِ نسكر نشعا تكو نزبابوروا
شنا برك دجونه جلشر لوا صراطى بدبا شكا كو عكو وا
اسا صر ريقننا نقد واد ملعى دسيلهو بر غدو سكر زاليا وا
سسا كم رينغننر تا التحريم شنا مو ننا دجمع النبا وا
قدا برو جيز نهم تا ابشك دليلى كوا اكر مع تنبيا وا
سهو كم زافما هك كودو اك شرا داكو نزبندر غكو وا
قيبا بر قدرو نحسترتا ابشك دلير كوا اكر مر تنبيدوا
محمد الرسول شنا غهشر ذو الجند داكر تبتدا وا
قا نبو بحر قا لجنا تنفقما شير ضوار شنا مرندد كووا
ششر كشعا كتبد غتر يفما غدر الجنة داكر تبنيا وا
قدا بر قباد خلو هدا تيا بشك دلير كوا اكر مر تنبيد وا
غدو ركر كو نز بندر ازر قد شسا كم فنة عنر كم تاب وا وا
وخلوا ازي اشدو زنا ابشك دلير كوا اكر مر تنبدوا
كدا اكم داكنز يا غو نه مرقبلر زضهر كاج داكر تبنسا وا

E.

ستهيرو فو زبير دباتر طوقا وهاتا يا ابن ياغن غكووا

وبقهكو كيتر شنى وتاد تشكر دبو سبير هد تا ابن غكووا

ششا غير دودهتر اغا زها تو زوتا ها ابن سوبا غكووا

صحه كم بنجى بجمع المسلم كذو ابن كيك بد زهوا ايا وا

ادو زشفا غدو النجنا بقبر انا بزغا انا مونا دكووا

ادهو سيلم كم دام توزيني تميلواد كي انا كم ز الثني ا وا

ادو زشكا ذبر قتونا دبونا انا زغدو زسيو ارد يا وي كووا

بدارشيك فو قبو بيتنم دزامينا انا مونا دجمع النبد وا

هلايكو اكذ ابد موسلينا بدارشك فوقبر احمد يا وي كووا

انا قبيرو قتوو انتر اتا شر زقوكم ذاط قو دزها ايا وا

بيرس

يشفا زشفا كا يراد نسر محمد هو امينه يا وي كووا

شمو كم كرنترا كه انس اپيشر ششعو ازسنا غبيا باوا

شمشا زشنا كم ير كرزار محمد اتر سو زد يا وي كو وا

انا كم بوسر الغيبز سر وتا ا مبو ذو ا غبا دزصر ايا وا

ابو بكري شنا دمشر محمد غمر غثمان شنا منا دكووا

كذا ى على طلحة هو زبير دسعد سلي كذ ام قبا ب وا

كذا بر غوف غامر غلشر تونا صحابر ذكى دجمع النبا وا

بذ كذا ر كوپر كو د زامينا انا مونا كذ ا غمرايا وا

ابنير غنذ ذاتر قلز سركيني دذ ا فوز شيك كو شكا وا

~~اهنتر كو د انجنا دنيه نيز شه بد نيز ابن نقم قصا~~

اهننه

F.

أمش كود الجنة نعما غر الله باشر اير غما وا

جنا ير شا رو فو هم تد ابنش دلير كو اكر مر تنبيا وا

أكو مو كم غا اتمنا ادو ما تمر حك باب متو را كو غكوو

قبل الله كسلام نكر جما غر محمد النبي نم ديا في كو وا

دند جت شكنو اكو ني نيثا مدينة عند احمد يدي كو وا

غدر كود نبرو انا سوكي كو دكو سوز رايه پار تاب وا وا

قبد ومر انا طوز ريه بلر جدر ند جر غا تهد يدي كو وا

بز بنا كنيم نيو او نغ وغطي ابو كيبت قز بنا ابا وا وا

كند وقبر وافد انا نوغطي نريش زمز هيمرا ابا بو وا وا

جنا غم وافد انا غود نم الله صحابة بدو وم غا نتهة يدي كو وا

تمت بحمد الله

وحسن عونه

والحمد لله رب

العالمين

m

G.1.

بسم الله الرحمن الرحيم وبه نستعين

يقاف نلابار سرا كنا ذاري ذغم

مالم موسى بن بيرى حنريذ وا

ذ امار عنقمار شي ذ امبا كوا

لا بار ذ عيكو الله اما ايصا اقا

تم تم موسو بيتي سروتا ذا اريا

ديذ ول بيبا كي ذ متا نو ذ اريا

بكورس سكوتا سكنوي

وسكو منغي سكذ منا

بيسا كنا اشي بيبيسو احر منغي

ذكي موطنش سكتا نش

سكنغي فسا غور سكو

غري انا شمش حبو جا اسكذ

منا شي بابا ونر يلا اشي

يتهي

عا مْ اَ سَا فَنْ كرانا اسا كلى نبى عمو نكر بيبى

عمرنا فونبى اسكا لكهنى اوسوا دكطا وقبى بيش

عك طر دوا بوا بيو ابا عوا ذو رعد غمر ودو يد

كاى يبا بيبى شيا نكرسبى كى ادوا ادوا يد

ربيرمشكى سكن عاقكر شسنو سوسا كلكى نوى

كى يام نوى مو كاشاكا كانرا ثانا

مو مو كو يكشا ابنا كو وكيبى شسنس كريد

شيبر سبر غو بيبيس بيكس يبا يرذ

كى ايا يرذ كى نتم ايد اوم وكوبيك س

شى اكرشيس ثربا انم عبريسك كى بياك

امام واقوم يبا ابا يرذ كى نتم ايبراس

شى بيكلى يبر موس مام بيرير ابنر اسوم مام

يا سكى يا كى بيبى ابا ارذ ثنا وسر

كى نحى اعك ربكيش يبا ابر نصر ثنى

سى وما بابا بابا بمتى ايا ارذ ثنا وسر

يا ارذ اعتنا وسر شتى بيم يبرالكنم عبد

G.3.

شيكر نسر تربتاشي يتلف منوري

بيياكي دسوأبيتي سربساكرتا

شي بيتفي باكي آجاب بيتي سرآككام

تسركي جاب آكيكاشي دغنا يكو

موآغ اريابيغ منا شيكر ابيوأبيتسا

بيساكر وتابتفي باكي آغوري

بيتي سربيكو موأبيغ منا شيكر الشر

تر ابيفت ينا ابيملو اعبد الكريم

ممماشاني بيتي سروتناذ اريا ببرنبرى

بيتاشي بيتفي باكي آغنتا نتا ابيما

بيبتي سربا بيكو موابيغ منا ابيسا

كرتاشي بيكوما بيتي سربابيكوم

بيغ منا ذاريا الله آذ ونشي . غموما

شا بيبوأعد آغنتا منا شا انر بيروكي

عمنغي الله بيتي سر سانر بابيكي

غنتا نتا ع بيتي سر تيكملاشي تيفي

اري وا

آرِي وا السَكُتُو أُبِيسَر آنَا بَاكِ بَابِنِي آنْرِكِي
يَاكِ آكَكِنْ عَشِي بِيَا آنَا آنْ مَشِ مَادَا كِي
بِيكُو كَامِنْيُوا الاعْنَا يَكُو مُو آغَرِيَا يَنْدَمَنَا
تَكِي سَرَوْتَنْشِي شُكَرَاشِ تَرَا يَا كِنْشِ هُدُ
بَا [illegible] يِمَنُوَاشِ سِيدِ بِنِي سَرَوْنَا دَارِيَا
دَبِشِي بِيشِ بَنْدَمِي بَا آشِغُودَ كُوهِي
آلمَهْرِي آبِرْنِي دَارِيَا سِيِشْبِكَاشِي مَكَنِ
بِيِي دَامَارِشِي سِيْبِشِي تَيكَا مْنَا آنْسِ
يَاكِ دَيِي سَوْبِيُوا أَبِيَاشِ يَنْلُوفِي
سَكُلُوا آكُوِدَنْشِي آنْكِي سَرَوْتَنْشِي
بَايِفْتُوَا سِيدِ آحْمَدَ آبِنِي سَرَوْنَا دَارِيَا
كُوِنْتَنْشِ تَمْسِي دَعْكَ تَنْكِي سَرَوْتَا
يِمَنُوَا بِيَا كِيَا آمْنَا نُودَ كَ آتْكِي
زَمْنِي شِرْ دَكَسَرْ آمَا آنَا نِ شِبْكِيتُوِيَا
كَبْطِيَا غْمْبِسَرْ عَ بِهَا دَكَرْ دَارِيُوا بَا آبِنْدِ
ذُبِيسَا آمِيكَا بَا بَا سَرَوْنَا مَمْدَا
عَبْدُ السَّلَامِ بِيسَرْكِي دَارِيَا شِيكُوَا

G.S.

بتوفي تياكي اكروا اكلبش دكيا
يمتوا ابينكومو باوتش تترا باه بيا
سركي عبد السلام عبد ييسركي دارنا
يبشكرا هوم شافد اشكر سروننا فر
كواسرو للاش يتاش يتف ياكي
اغونو اجيش سبا بيكومو ايكمنا
يشاكرتاش بلف باكي هدنند
كواونو سباكا فر ديتيش اككاموا
دكاكذو دلاش غمتيش اكينكاانر
بايونزياكي بتاش بتف كوفنكي
نيباكي دكي بيكومو ايدمنا بيسا
كنلاش بتف ورص فرنباكي دشتي
دسزكي كنوا عبد الله وسكني بربار
ونزباكي بيساكر ياكي فدوا بيشكرا
غومتشافد تكرسروتا اكيفنشر
يابيغنوا اسركي عبد ابو بكر بيني لسرو
تاغرايا سلا يلاتر بيفي بهاكي اغدو

بيلي مر

بِتْ مُرْ شُكَرَ اَلَّهْ بِبُوا اَدُو تَا بِيَرْ بِيمُوا اُيَا بِهُلُوا
اَبُو بَكَرْ عَبْدُ بِكُوا اِنْكَرْ سَرُوْنَا شُكَرَ اَلِرْ بِيَرْ
دُوْ تَا بِيَرْ اَاكِبِنْتِي مُرْ بَا اِفِنُوا عَبْدُ سُنْبُ
بِتْ سَرُوْنَا اَدَارْ بَا بَاَ مُرْ بِتِيفِي بَالِكِي
اَبِيرِ بِيفِي سَرْ بِكُو مُوا اَيْ اَمْنَا بِلَا اكِرْ
تَا اَاشِ يَنْفِ كُنْتُرُ بِنْ سَرْ بِكُو سُوا
بِنْ اَمْنَا بِسَا اكِرْ تَاشِ يَنْفِ يَا اكِي
اَفِ بَا بِتِيشِبَا بِكُو مُوا اَيْ اَمْنَا بِسَا
كِرْ بَاشِ بِنْفِ يَا اكِي مُبَدُ اَلِسَا
بِهِلِي سِرْ بَا اِكُو مُوا اَيْدَ مَنَا اُيكِرْ
سَرُوْ تَا اَنَسْ شُبَكَرَ اَشِرْ تَرَ دُوْ تَا
شِدْ اَكِبْلَا اَشِ اَاسَرُوْ نِيشِ بَا
سُنْبُ شِنَا دَ شُكَرَ اَدُوْ تُكُسْ دُوْ نَا
شِدْ اَنِبِيَا رَانَا اَلْغَمَسْ اُمْنِتَا وَ اسُكَرُوْ
اَغَ اَرِ بَا عُمَرُ نُبَا اكِي سُكَشِي مُتَابِرْ
غَارِ بَا دَ بَلَا اَنْكَرْ سَرُوْنَا سَرْكِي تُنْبُ
بَا بَا اَفِنْدَ سُنْبُ عُثْمَانْ بِنْ سَرُوْنَا

G.7.

كاريبا اشناد ووتا بيرو ۞ انكر سرو نا ايتا شني
يتف ياكى اوفي ابيث سريكو ناكمرز ۞ ديكومو
يتو منا يسا كتاش يتف ركبا بياكى
كسو اينيثي سبا يكومو ايا منا يسا كريتا
شى يتف ككفر بيتفى سبا يكومو اينه منا يسا
كتاش يتف ٤٦ اكلو ايثى سريكومو ايتا منا
يسا كتاكتاش يتف ياكى اكنذ ايتى
سريكومو ايكا منا يتا ۞ يف يتا شريتف
ياكى ابوجا ييكومو با ييثى سبها
يا كنش شدا
ونزلا بارى سراكتا ذوو ريا السوغوم
شا بيوانتذ غ مالم موسر بهريا
حربيذو اعتمار نينذ دياكوكى
ذ لشكر ونزلا بارى عنفاتشرى
ونز لنا ف تا
تكا يسر بيرذ ا
الله

بسم الله الرحمن الرحيم
صلى الله على من لا نبي بعده

	١٥	[illegible]	[illegible]	٧	١١	١٤	[illegible]
	٩	[illegible]	[illegible]	١٧	[illegible]	[illegible]	[illegible]
[illegible]	٨	١٨	[illegible]	[illegible]	[illegible]	[illegible]	[illegible]
[illegible]	[illegible]	[illegible]	[illegible]	[illegible]	[illegible]	[illegible]	١
[illegible]	[illegible]	[illegible]	[illegible]	[illegible]	[illegible]	[illegible]	[illegible]
[illegible]	[illegible]	[illegible]	[illegible]	[illegible]	[illegible]	[illegible]	[illegible]
[illegible]	[illegible]	[illegible]	[illegible]	[illegible]	[illegible]	[illegible]	[illegible]

وتقرأ آية الكرسي سبعة

For EU product safety concerns, contact us at Calle de José Abascal, 56–1°, 28003 Madrid, Spain or eugpsr@cambridge.org.

www.ingramcontent.com/pod-product-compliance
Ingram Content Group UK Ltd.
Pitfield, Milton Keynes, MK11 3LW, UK
UKHW010047140625
459647UK00012BB/1661